Healing The Earth
...a time for change

to our
fearless
leaders
from the
unlimited Ron
oo

Enjoy! Blessings to
you from the heart!
☺ Kathryn
Lund

JOHN SANDFORD
& MARK SANDFORD

Healing The Earth...A Time For Change

© 2013 John Sandford & Mark Sandford

Printed by BT Johnson Publishing

Battle Ground, WA 98604

www.btjohnsonpublishing.com

ISBN # 978-1-938311-01-7

Cover Design by Talan Warden

JOHN   MARK

SANDFORD & SANDFORD

Healing
The
Earth

...a time for change

Contents

Acknowledgements

Our first acknowledgement is to our Heavenly Father, His Son—the Lord Jesus Christ, and the Holy Spirit, without whose wisdom, saving grace, example and inspiration, the revelations and writing of this book could never have happened.

We also want to acknowledge our debt to all the saints throughout Christian history. Doing the research made us keenly aware of our continuity with all who have gone before. We stand on the shoulders of those whose stories thrilled us and became powerful testimonies in the book.

Many thanks to the board members and advisors of Elijah House who read our rough draft and generated helpful critiques, edits and revisions. We are grateful because it taught us once again that two minds are better than one, and three or more is infinitely better. The Lord does not want solitary saints, but those who can hear and cherish and help hone their brothers' efforts.

We thank and acknowledge the many members and friends who listened to oral teaching on the subject and gave input that caused us to revise our thinking before a word was ever written.

This book is the product of many hearts and minds. We are glad to acknowledge that.

I (John) particularly want to acknowledge the genius of our son Mark, whose biblical clarity, strictly orthodox beliefs and ability to restate what could have been misunderstood, turned a good book into what I now think is a great and needed manuscript for the Body of Christ.

i

Finally, I want to acknowledge and give thanks to my many family members who, for at least ten years, have had to call out so many times, "Earth to Dad" (and "Grandkids to Granddad") while I wrestled with how to express many things. It's such a relief, now that the book is done, to be able to be more present to all whom I love and who love me.

Foreword By John Paul Jackson

The Earth is a wonderful and mysterious planet. It is unique and one of a kind. In all of creation, no other sphere contains the beauty and variety of life this planet does. Yet, in all its beauty, it is quite strange. While its crust is solid, its core is molten, and in spite of our great technological advances, no one is exactly sure of the core's composition. Not only is the core molten, it rotates at a different speed than its crust, and we have no idea why.

We do know that, due to the extreme heat within the earth's core, it needs the four seasons to keep from over-heating. So it is good that the Earth has seasonal wobbles, and that the whole Earth does not experience winter or summer at the same time. There are so many simple matters about the Earth that are wonderful, but remain a quandary to man.

Science tells us there are four basic forces that govern the physical interactions of all matter, but it doesn't know why these four — gravity, electro-static presence, strong nuclear bonds and weak nuclear bonds—work together. We do know that when they are in balance they form a "user-friendly" environment filled with order and stability — as long as humans work together with it. As simple as this may sound, no one understands the entirety of the divine, grand logic behind how each of these forces work.

We seldom think about the simplest of the four, which is gravity, and how it holds down everything on Earth. Think about it; what if gravity let go? And how does gravity hold humans down to the Earth anyway? Magnets work on metal, but skin,

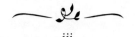

that's a whole new thought. We aren't even sure what gravity is and what is its composition. Someone might say, "Gravity is made of gravitons." But what are gravitons? The truth is, no one knows.

There are many mysteries that most of us don't know exist. Another such mystery is that plants grow very well when some types of classical music are played to them during the day. Still more mysterious is that they grow faster and stronger when the sound of chirping birds is played. Who would have thought that the morning and evening sound of their chirping actually helps the earth produce life?

Not only does the earth respond to bird life, it responds to all forms of life — especially human life. It is as if we who were formed from the dust of the earth are to interact in some way that allows creation to respond to the presence of God in us. We may not fully know why creation works the way it does, but this we do know: creation responds to us, to our presence, to our weaknesses, to our strengths, and even to our mistakes. All of creation looks to mankind for the fulfillment of its purpose.

We go about our daily lives giving little thought to what we are walking on, let alone how this grand and beautiful design of God works. But the Bible does speak about creation and our role in it far more than we think. Some of the thoughts the Bible reveals are puzzles, some are enigmas, and others seem inconsequential until the consequence of that which once seemed insignificant occurs. Here too we have ignored or overlooked our God-directed role in the earth fulfilling its purpose.

You start seeing some odd things when you look past the traditional understanding of Scripture and consider it in fresh

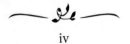

ways. We find that the stones and trees have music, animals can speak, and that the earth can yield or refuse to yield crops to us, almost as if it has some mysterious wisdom of its own.

The Apostle Paul seemed to believe that the earth is more than inanimate soil, stone, water, and foliage. He seemed to believe that the earth has memory, and some sort of ability of *choice* — that is, some ability of will. Perhaps it is not a "will" as we currently understand will, but clearly, there is something going on in Romans 8 that suggests the earth has expectations, it feels futility, it hopes, it groans and it has some form of desire to fulfill its purpose. Perhaps the First Nations people (the American Indians) and the Jewish sages are correct; the earth does work with man. It does remember every footprint that walks upon it, and every word spoken is still reverberating through out creation.

If the earth has all this, as Paul apparently thought, does it therefore have a choice about when, how, and to whom it yields itself? If lack of righteousness caused the earth not to yield its strength to the likes of Adam and Cain, does a greater presence of righteousness allow creation to work in tandem with mankind?

This concept may be somewhat "metaphysical" in nature, but perhaps it is time for the Church to come to a clearer understanding of the biblical order of creation — how God created us to function, how He created the earth to function, and how the two are meant to function together in harmony.

There is a reason why God did not simply speak us into existence, as He did the vegetation, the animals, the moon and the stars. Instead, He chose to create us out of the earth. He shaped us from the soil and then breathed His breath into us.

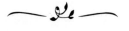

Why would He do that? Could it be that humans are to have a relationship with the earth, and the earth is to have a relationship with us that we don't yet understand? Could it be that just as it was with Cain, our choices affect the earth? Could this be a reason why God said the day will come when He will judge those who destroy the earth (Revelation 11:18)?

Perhaps when we walk in greater righteousness, we will see the earth "yield its strength" (Genesis 4:12) to us in unexpected and remarkable ways. What would that look like? With the assistance of his son, Mark, John Sandford tackles many of these puzzling issues in this brilliant, insightful and seasoned approach to what the Bible tells us is to be our relationship with all of creation. Some of what John writes will shock you, some will surprise you, and all of it will make you think more deeply about God and what He intended when He created mankind, the Heavens, and the Earth.

In reading *Healing the Earth*, you will come away with a greater appreciation for what God put mankind here to do. You will discover that our purpose for being here is tied to all of creation in unexpected ways. You will become painfully aware that while the Earth was created to help mankind; mankind was also created to help the Earth, which began to languish the moment Adam sinned. Until righteousness returns in a greater measure than we are currently seeing, all of creation will continue to "groan" (Romans 8:22), and mankind will miss so much of what God intended us to experience on this amazing planet called Earth.

Foreword By James Goll

Pioneers always take new territory — they are never settlers. John Sandford has been, and remains, one of the greatest Christian forerunners in recent church history. It has been one of my great honors to know and walk with this dear man of God over the recent years. I fondly refer to him as "Uncle John."

In the early seventies, caught up in the Jesus People Movement, I began praying daily for the School of the Prophets to come forth. I prayed for nearly a decade for such a thing to take place. Then, finally, I was given a copy of a book called, *The Elijah Task*. Little did I know at the time that the book I held in my hand would drastically shape my life. It gave me sanity as a young man. It gave me hope and defined with uncanny wisdom who I was and what I was called to do with the rest of my life.

I thank the Lord for the trail-blazing that the team ministry of John and Paula Sandford have done that has altered the course of church history present and shaped that which is yet to come.

You have in your hands another treatise, another scholarly book, yes, and another pioneering work. Like his early works, some will shout its praises and others might temporarily sit in the seat of the scoffer—to only later, down the road, realize they were being given an opportunity to expand their understanding and grow in the redemptive revelation of the fullness of God's plan for mankind. This book pioneers another frontier.

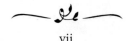

As for me, when I read this manuscript, I was amazed, enlightened, expanded, thrilled, and my heart even skipped a beat a time or two. Just think — God wants to heal the land! God wants His kingdom to come and His will to be done on earth as it is in heaven. If I remember correctly, I read somewhere that if we confessed our sins and repented of our wicked ways, God would forgive our sins and "heal our land." Is that really a part of God's redemptive plan? Yes, the very earth cries out for healing.

Healing the Earth builds on the progressive, revelatory truths the Holy Spirit has released in recent decades. Truths like confessing generational sins, identificational repentance, reconciliation, praying by prophetic unction, depending on the now voice of the Holy Spirit, taking dominion, impacting the "seven cultural mountains" and many more. This book leaps into the future of God's highest will and brings glimpses of it within the grasp of our now.

Now we are given a model that truly reveals, "All things are possible." It is with my utmost respect and deepest honor that I now commend to you the writings of one of the most dedicated men of the heart, integrated with one of the most intelligent minds in recent church history, as well as that of his son, Mark, who joins him as co-author. John Sandford exudes the mind of Christ, and loves his Lord and Savior with all his heart.

It has been my joy and honor, in my own personal pilgrimage of faith, for the shadow of this great man of God to touch my personal life. With honor to whom honor is due, I commend to you the man of God and the transforming truths he and Mark have been given to steward in the classic book, *Healing the Earth*.

Introduction

This book has been more than ten years in the writing. There were so many questions and problems. The first was, "Should I (John) build a scientific basis for *Healing the Earth*, or should I address the subject personally, more by story and testimony?" After pondering and praying, I felt led by the Holy Spirit not to go the scientific route. The Lord made it clear that our target is not the intelligentsia. We do not write to those who wait to be scientifically convinced that the earth needs to be healed. We write primarily to those who are already believing and obedient, but who have long wondered how to walk out that obedience. In some ways, this is a "how to" book.

But that raised a second question: "In our lifetime, to what extent does God want to set creation free from its bondage to decay?" As the reader will see (in the 8th chapter, "The Enemy — Us!"), I realized that if many people rushed too quickly to liberate the creation while mankind remained coarse and insensitive, it would be more wounding to nature than if nothing were done. Furthermore, the Lord has made it clear in His Word that only after He reveals the sons of God at the time of our resurrection, will the creation be completely set free (Romans 8:19-23). This book is a preparation for that glorious time. It teaches how to heal specific animals, plants, objects, lands and nations, but not how to set the entire creation free from its bondage to decay. That awaits the second coming.

Consequently, a third question arose: Matthew 17:11 says that Elijah shall come and restore "all things" before the

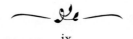

Lord returns. But how much does "all" mean? Many Scriptures indicate, and most scholars believe, that things will get worse before He returns, not better. How much of creation, therefore, is to be restored before He returns? The reader will see that we could not, and did not, try to answer these questions. But we do insist that we are to respond to His call to be found doing His will when He comes — that is, in the healing of the earth as well as in all other areas of our calling — evangelism, teaching, healing people, etc. We just don't know what the call to restore "all things" really means. Before the second coming, to what extent can restoration come to the earth's governments? Politics? The Church? Nature? This book simply calls us to obey Him, to keep doing the specific things He has shown us to do — until He returns.

This book is intended to call forth the testimonies and labors of many throughout the Body of Christ, but not to entertain with more stories than necessary. Many have experienced far greater revelations and healings of the earth than we have. Therefore, I (John) was faced with a decision: should I include their testimonies? The Lord guided me not to do so. He didn't want the book to be too long. If responses are good, I may write a sequel with little else than the testimonies of many who have been called to the healing of the earth.

A great problem is that, although the healing of the earth should always have been the province of Christians, we have been tardy in responding. Nature abhors a vacuum. New Agers have so occupied and defiled the field that many Christians are afraid of being labeled (or libeled, as the case may be) as New Agers. Many have become afraid to venture and learn wisdom by trial and error. This book is a call to courage, to trust the Lord's

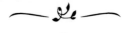

grace, to be willing to risk what people think, and to be able to withstand our own stumbling and errors in learning how to do what is necessary. Our purpose is to enlist all who have faith, and who hunger for the healing of the earth, into the enterprise of serving and discovering. When the sons of God hear the call, that which forerunners like myself and others have learned will be at hand, and those who have been called will know what to do — and how to do it.

Perhaps the greatest problem I faced is what I will say repeatedly throughout the book:

If God's people are to be obedient to the call to heal animals, plants, objects, lands and nations, then entire paradigms of thought, ingrained in us as we have grown up, will have to be overturned and abandoned for more Hebraic and biblical ways of thinking, seeing and acting.

This book is therefore a call to humility of mind. On the one hand, to hang on determinedly to the core of what is biblically right and orthodox. On the other, to see that some of the ways we have thought and acted (and called "biblical") are, in fact, erroneous. The book is a summons to flexibility and willingness to move beyond our comfort zones for a calling which may abrogate old ways of thinking that we have become accustomed to regarding as "biblical." I suspect that our readers are already that type of Christian, else they would not have picked up this book. Let us form a company of intercessors and doers until that day when our Lord says, "Okay, have at it. It's time to set the creation free from its bondage to decay."

CHAPTER ONE

THE CALL

ost thou think that…the plants and brute creatures here below should serve thy uses only, and maintain thy life by their own death and destruction?…Surely thou canst not think so. For thou art…the means or instrument whereby the rest of the inferior creatures make their recourse unto that God from whom they originally proceeded (author unknown, from a sermon entitled, "The Book of Nature," 1686).[1][2]

---

[1] Boys, Richard C., Ralph Cohen, Vinton A. Dearing and Lawrence Clark Powell, editors, *Theologia Ruris, Sive Schola Et Scalla Naturae (The Book of Nature)*, (Los Angeles, CA: William Andrews Clark Memorial Library and the University of California, 1956), 198-199.

[2] **Note:** in 1686, *The Book of Nature* was attached to the end of *The History of Hai Eb'n Yockdan, an Indian Prince: Or the Self-Taught Philosopher*, a book that promoted Enlightenment philosophy. However, it had no connection to this book or its philosophy. Rather, "The Book of Nature" was originally a stand-alone sermon that reflected an attitude toward nature common among Christians at the turn of the eighteenth century (p. 1 of the introduction).

Healing The Earth

When I (Mark) was seven years old, my family vacationed in a postcard-perfect clapboard cottage in the gentle wilds of New Hampshire. On a morning walk down a sun-dappled lane, I came upon a jovial old soul trying her best to entice chipmunks to eat out of her hand.

"Can I try?" I whispered timidly.

"I dunno," she hedged. "I've been at it for a day and a half, and they're still too skittish to come clear up to me." But, to spare my feelings, she humored me with a handful of sunflower seeds and went inside to putter around her Norman Rockwell kitchen. Within minutes, skittering balls of fluff were snatching treats from my outstretched palms, and my newfound friend was clutching the phone at her gingham-curtained window, effervescing to my Mom that she had just witnessed a moment in Eden.

Years later, God's creatures were not as eager to trust me. I fully understood why. In our household, it was common knowledge that they shy away from a hardening heart. If I was ever to enjoy another moment like that, I would have to allow God to peel back the layers of bitterness that had since distanced me from God's heart. And I would have to learn again how to eat out of His hand.

As I contemplate that small loss, I can only imagine what the common ancestor of us all must have felt about his loss. Poor Adam. He and his Creator had enjoyed daily walks infinitely more intoxicating than my little morning stroll. When Adam fell, he had to watch his sickness creep over paradise like a cancerous rash. Pets who once ate from his hand fled in terror, and ripped each other apart. Adam had effortlessly

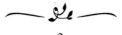

tilled a garden that stretched beyond every horizon. Now he struggled to extract a living from among the thorns (Genesis 3:18). "What have I done?" he must have anguished. "I have spoiled everything! I am exiled, and none who come after me will ever know the sweetness of the earth I once loved!"

Poor Cain. After murdering his brother, Abel, he must have cried, "What have I done? At least my father still reaped bounty among the thorns. But for me the earth '…will no longer yield its strength'" (Genesis 4:12, All Scriptures NAS unless otherwise specified.)! "My father was exiled from Eden, but I am exiled from God. 'Today You are driving me from the land and I will be hidden from Your presence'" (Genesis 4:14, NIV). From then on, he had to watch his descendants sweat in the stifling sun, weeding thistles from paltry plots of stubborn ground.

Poor us! Even in their darkened state, Adam and Cain could not have helped but see how their sin ruined the earth — the change took place before their very eyes. Although we are aware of the ways we pollute it physically, do we know that our sin pollutes it spiritually? The answer became clear when I asked a scholarly friend to review this book's original draft. He predicted that readers would ask, "Why a book on healing the earth? Won't it distract from the central message of salvation? What does the cross have to do with this?" I added this chapter in response to these questions. (My father penned the remaining chapters which, with his assistance, I edited and expanded with research and stories that brought perspective and color to an already rich manuscript.)

As I wrote, it occurred to me that the very fact that we have to ask such questions reveals how far we have strayed from the

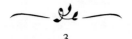

truth that rang so painfully in the ears of Adam and Cain — that our sin is no private matter! The state of our hearts is the state of the land on which we live. In Leviticus 18:25 (NIV), God says, "Even the land was defiled; **so I punished it for its sin**, and the land vomited out its inhabitants" (emphasis added). What strange wording! "**Its** sin!" Does that mean the land can choose to sin? Of course not! It means that sin pollutes the land just as surely as the Valdez oil spill sullied Alaska's pristine coastline. Our sin becomes "its sin," and the land takes the punishment along with us.

Are you beginning to see how central is the cross to this issue? Only the cross can save us from our sins.

By extension, only the cross can save the land from the spiritual pollution by which we blight it!

There are those who have discovered that the land does not have to take its full punishment, if only we would allow the cross to have its way with us. In the wake of World War II, Mother Basilea Schlink and her companions were building a center near Darmstat, Germany to house their newly established evangelical sisterhood. After a dump-cart loaded with sand derailed six times, Basilea discerned that their vindictive attitudes were affecting the physical world around them. She urged her sisters to repent and reconcile with each other and with God, and the cart never jumped its tracks again. From then on, by the same means they periodically stopped torrential rains, frost and heat waves that hindered the building process.[3] For Basilea, the abstract idea that sin spiritually pollutes the

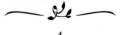

land became concrete reality!

There came a day when God convicted Mother Basilea to stop polluting the land physically as well. At God's prompting, she insisted that her ministry cease using pesticides. Some of her sisters complained that this "defied all common sense," but Basilea felt convicted that repentance would be the most effective pesticide. They began picking off inchworms and catching rabbits by hand. As tedious as this seemed, Basilea chose to view the hard work of practicing such kindness to the earth as an indication of their willingness to bend to God's will.

Her staff continued to combine these efforts with repentance, both individually and as a group, for whatever sins God revealed. The Lord tested them with a season of drought, but they persevered. So He rewarded them with refreshing rains, along with ladybugs to eat plant lice, birds to pick off insects, and human helpers to assist with weeding. The result was a harvest so copious that they were able to feed not only themselves and their guests, but also needy families in the nearby town!

They dubbed that summer, "the time of unmasking." This was repeated year after year (usually without the drought), as again and again God sternly alerted Mother Basilea and her companions to cleanse their hearts. Every time insects invaded their garden they dropped their tools, retreated to their rooms and asked the Holy Spirit to reveal whatever sin had invited the pests. In every case, after repenting and reconciling they returned to their garden and found that the pests had moved out.[4]

[3] Schlink, Mother Basilea, *Repentance, the Joy Filled Life* (Minneapolis, MN: Bethany House Publishers, 1968), 67-68.

[4] Schlink, Mother Basilea, *A Matter of Life and Death* (Darmstadt-Everstadt, Germany: Evangelical Sisterhood of Mary, 1974), 343-345.

Healing The Earth

Sometimes the unmasking was painful, but the bountiful results produced great faith, even in those who normally tended toward discouragement!

Since Scripture says that God "…sends rain on the righteous and the unrighteous" (Matthew 5:45), I caution that not every natural occurrence is due to sin. But today's way of thinking blinds many Christians to the possibility that it ever is. I wonder if, for some who live a repentant lifestyle, nature has responded and they have chalked it up to mere coincidence. What an added incentive to live like Jesus they might have missed!

Even if we all do as Mother Basilea did, in this life we will not restore the earth altogether. Only in the new Earth will "…the creation itself…be liberated from its bondage to decay and brought into the glorious freedom of the children of God" (Romans 8:21, NIV). But to whatever extent we step into that freedom in our lifetime, earth will reap the benefits, just as surely as it has reaped the consequences of our captivity to sin. Israel discovered this principle anew every time repentance ended a drought, famine or plague. Ezekiel and Isaiah prophesied:

> On the day that I shall have cleansed you from all your iniquities…the desolate land will be cultivated instead of being a desolation in the sight of everyone who passes by. They will say, "This desolate land has become **like the garden of Eden**" (Ezekiel 37:33a, 34-35a, emphasis added).

> Her wilderness He will make **like Eden**, and her desert **like the garden of the LORD** (Isaiah 51:3, emphasis added).

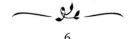

Of course Ezekiel and Isaiah didn't mean that Israel would literally regain the full flowering of Eden. But they did mean that for those who lead a lifestyle of repentance, Eden's blessings are not entirely irretrievable.

This is not a long-lost principle that Mother Basilea rediscovered after 2,000 years of disuse. Throughout history, saints have lived out this truth. It is a little known fact that many of them experienced a bit of Eden in their lifetimes. For instance, in second century Asia Minor (modern day Turkey), by his prayers St. Albercius created a warm spring that healed the sick.[5] In fourth century Egypt, St. John the dwarf watered a dry stick until it sprouted, grew into a tree, and bore fruit.[6] In sixth century Palestine, St. Mastridia went to the wilderness to pray. For seventeen years her small basket of beans never ran out although she never replenished it, and her clothing never wore out.[7] In ninth century Greece, by prayer, St. Daniel drove all the snakes out of the island of Thasos.[8] In tenth century Greece, St. Luke of Hellas went to his field to plant wheat. Along the way he gave more than half of his seed to the poor, but God rewarded him with a greater harvest than the entire amount would have produced.[9] During the same century, three anonymous women were able to devote their lives to full-time prayer in the Greek wilderness for eleven years because birds continually brought them food.[10] In fourteenth Century Russia,

[5] Velimirovic, St. Nicholai, *The Prologue of Ohrid, Volume 2* (Alhambra, CA: Serbian Orthodox Diocese of North America, 2002), 457.
[6] Velimirovic, *Vol. 2*, 523.
[7] Velimirovic, *Vol. 2*, 137.
[8] Velimirovic, *Vol. 2*, 297.
[9] Velimirovic, *Vol. 1*, 137.
[10] Velimirovic, *Vol. 2*, 290-291.

the Orthodox St. Paul of Obnora kept company with foxes and a bear who refused to harm the birds, rabbits and other small animals who also attended him.[11] In early seventeenth century America, a three-month drought in New England suddenly ended when Protestant pilgrims spent just nine hours in prayers of repentance for greed and lack of concern for their fellow men.[12] Late in the same century, an extreme infestation of caterpillars ravaged their great-grandchildren's crops. The Puritans repented of their spiritual sloth, idolatry and self-sufficiency, and the plague instantly ceased.[13] In early twentieth century Russia, the Orthodox Fr. Kuksha was fed by a raven, just like Elijah at the Kerith Brook (1 Kings 17:6).[14] In late twentieth century Greece, when two bears charged toward the Orthodox Elder Paisios on his way to market, they suddenly halted. He fed them each a piece of bread he had blessed, then led them into town, where — to the amazement of the townspeople — he loaded provisions on their backs, which they happily carried back to his monastery![15/16]

Some believers question the title, "Saint," because we are all called to be saints, and there are no second-class citizens in the Kingdom. Our sentiments exactly! If we indulge the capital

---

[11] Stefanatos, Joanne, D.V.M., *Animals and Man: a State of Blessedness* (Minneapolis, MN: Light and Life Publishing Co.,1992), 262-263.

[12] Marshall, Peter and David Manuel, *The Light and the Glory* (Old Tappan, NJ: Fleming H. Revell Co., 1977), 142.

[13] Marshall, and Manuel, 217.

[14] Stefanatos, 204.

[15] Markides, Kyriacos C., *The Mountain of Silence* (New York, NY: Doubleday — Random House, Inc., 2002), 93.

[16] **Note:** saints specified here as "Orthodox" lived after the Catholic/Orthodox split in the mid-eleventh century. Earlier saints mentioned are recognized by both Catholics and Orthodox.

"S," it is to keep us from forgetting their extraordinary examples. But these very ordinary people simply showed us what any ordinary saint should be doing. There is no reason why our experience should be unlike theirs, if only our walk would be as radically committed. Sainthood is not a luxury for the few!

As the everyday saints around me grow in the Lord, little blessings reveal just how relevant is healing the earth to the work of the cross. As a teenager, I watched my father cultivate our town's most profuse garden. "How do you do it?" neighbors asked with jaws agape. "We used the same nutrients and planting methods as you." The answer was simple. My Dad walked with Jesus, and he prayed for his garden. We once got nine pickings from a single crop of peas! The whole neighborhood found out, and many people were challenged to consider that Jesus is real, and that therefore, His work on the cross might be relevant to their lives.

My wife, Maureen, has created a mini-Eden in our dining room. Vines carpet the entire ceiling and grow so rapidly that if she does not trim them often, they begin to hang down, and people joke that you need a machete to find your way through! If Maureen's vines begin to sicken, the Holy Spirit reveals it to her before they show signs of wilting. She digs them up and, sure enough, little bugs are nibbling at the roots. She repots them, and they rebound with such gusto that friends ask what "miracle" plant food she's been using! A friend gave her a tropical plant and told her to expect it to bloom once every seven years. For Maureen, it blooms every three weeks! To visitors, God seems a little closer after relaxing in her little indoor garden.

Healing The Earth

Nature is a means through which God reveals His glory, and we are a means through which God enables nature to cooperate with Him.

Years ago, while ministering in Taiwan (after years of peeling back my layers of bitterness), I took a baby-step toward regaining my childhood ability to act as such a means. Staff members complained that mosquitoes wouldn't let them sleep. Then I thought to myself, "Surely God's original intention for these creatures was not that they should torment us! And if Jesus commanded the wind and waves to be still, in His name I should at least be able command mosquitoes not to bite." Not wanting to act presumptuously, I asked God for permission before commanding them in Jesus' name to stay away. The next morning I awakened unblemished from a dreamless sleep, while a baggy-eyed co-worker in the next room scratched tiny red blotches from head to toe. We all swore that from then on we would never forget what God commanded Adam and Eve: "Fill the earth, and subdue it; and rule over the fish of the sea and over the birds of the sky and over every living thing that moves on the earth" (Genesis 1:28).

Although God drove Adam and Eve from the garden, He did not revoke our dominion over the earth. Rather, it is we who compromise it.

I pray that God turns our baby-steps into the full stride of spiritual adulthood. Oh, to be more like Jesus! For in the days to come, as increasing sin reaps increasing turmoil in the natural

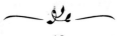

world, we'll need to exercise dominion over much greater things. Like Jesus, may we calm the storms to come, and may our lives, homes and farms provide a bit of Eden that beckons a wayward world back to the cross and to purity of heart.

I have been using the word, "Eden," loosely. I am not suggesting, as New Agers do, that we need to get "**back** to the garden" and become like "the first Adam." Rather, as St. Ephraim the Syrian said in the mid-fourth century, "The diligent…now run **forward** to meet paradise as it exults with every sort of fruit. They enter the garden with glorious deeds"[17] (emphasis added). As we wait for our future home in the new earth (Revelation 21:1), we must recognize that Christ, whom Paul dubbed, "the last Adam" (1 Corinthians 15:45), has the commission "… to reconcile to Himself [not only us, but] **all things**, whether **things on earth** or things in heaven, by making peace through His blood, shed on the cross" (Colossians 1:20, NIV, emphasis added). By extension, Christ's sacrifice for us benefits His entire creation and gives us a foretaste of life in the world to come, in the company of a Savior whose loving presence will make it a much richer garden than the one we lost.

As His ambassadors we share His ministry of reconciliation, not only with fellow humans, but with the earth as well.

Some might ask, "But why should we bother to heal the earth if it's going to be burned up anyway?" This very question reveals our selfishness! If we seek to heal our ailing bodies even

---

[17] Guroian, Vigen, *Inheriting Paradise, Meditations on Gardening* (Grand Rapids MI: Wm. B. Eerdman's Publishing Co., 1999), 39.

though they will eventually die, should we not do the same for God's ailing Earth, although it will also die? If we do not steward this Earth well, what will we do with a new one? Would you trust your child with a thousand dollars if he has foolishly squandered the five you already gave him? In his book, *Pollution and the Death of Man*, Francis Schaeffer said:

> The Christian who believes the Bible should be the man who — with God's help and in the power of the Holy Spirit — is treating nature now in the direction of the way nature will be then [after Christ returns]. It will not now be perfect, but there should be something substantial or we have missed our calling. God's calling to the Christian now, and to the Christian community, in the area of nature (just as it is in the area of personal Christian living in true spirituality) is that we should exhibit a substantial healing here and now, between man and nature and nature and itself, as far as Christians can bring it to pass.[18]

This earth is a school where we learn to exercise dominion as Jesus does — as servant-rulers. How will we serve the earth? Will we value, heal and transform it? Or will we use it for selfish gain? Dr. Schaeffer also said:

> God treats His creation with integrity...If God treats His creation in that way...shouldn't I, as a fellow creature, do the same? ...And for the highest reason: because I

---

[18] Schaeffer, Francis and Udo Middelmann, *Pollution and the Death of Man* (Wheaton, IL: Tyndale Publishing, 1970), 67.

love God — I love the One who has made it! Loving the Lover who has made it, I have respect for the thing He has made.[19]

My father and I will not write about conservation, recycling and other means of physical stewardship. Plenty of authors more scientifically qualified have already covered that ground. Instead, we'll focus on a forgotten principle few have talked about — that just as the earth fell with us, it can be restored to whatever degree we are restored, through our prayers and our continual transformation into the likeness of Christ (2 Corinthians 3:18).

To that end, dear saint, we challenge you to ask yourself, "Is the earth blossoming around me?" "Does it yield its produce for me?" "Are animals (both domestic and wild) loving and gentle in my presence?"

2 Corinthians 3:18 says, "But we all, with unveiled face, beholding as in a mirror the glory of the Lord, are being transformed into the same image from glory to glory, just as from the Lord, the Spirit." As your transforming soul increasingly reflects God's glory, the earth around you should reflect this even more than it once reflected your corruption. The extent to which it does may be a good measure of the extent to which you have been transformed! Anestis Keselopoulos[20] has

---

[19] Schaeffer and Middelmann, 67.
[20] **Note:** Professor Keselopoulos is a devout Orthodox Christian and the Director of the Department of Ethics and Sociology at Aristotle University of Thessaloniki in Thessaloniki, Greece.

said, "The church fathers[21] insistently maintain that a person is characterized as virtuous or vicious according to his relationship with the things of creation and the way he uses them."[22]

It is time to return to that forgotten standard. As we daily pray, "Your will be done, *on earth* as it is in heaven" (Matthew 6:10, emphasis added), let's really mean it. Let us serve Jesus — and His good earth — as He serves us. Let us heal as He heals.

---

[21] **Note:** that is, saints and theologians of the past — with regard to the subject being discussed, in the western church, at least until the 1300's; in the eastern church, until the present.
[22] Keselopoulos, Anestis G., *Man and His Environment* (Crestwood, NY: St. Vladimir's Seminary Press, 2001), 90.

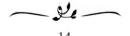

CHAPTER TWO

THE GLORY

"God is love" (I John 4:8). Everything He does is an expression of His loving nature. Therefore, God created the earth in love, and for love. All of earth, all its objects and creatures, are redolent with God's loving nature. Since the fall of man and the subsequent curse upon nature, the whole earth has been subject to corruption (Romans 8:21), no longer able to express the Creator's love in the fullness for which our Lord fashioned it.

Ability and Desire to Worship God

God created earth to praise Him, and He gave it capacity to do so, which it still retains:

The heavens are telling the glory of God; and their expanse is declaring the work of His hands.

Psalm 19:1

Praise the Lord!

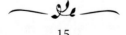

Healing The Earth

Praise the Lord from the heavens;
Praise Him in the heights!
Praise Him, all His angels;
Praise Him, all His hosts!
Praise Him, sun and moon;
Praise Him, all stars of light!
Praise Him, highest heavens,
And the waters that are above the heavens!
Let them praise the name of the Lord.
For He commanded and they were created.
He has established them forever and ever;
He has made a decree which will not pass away.

Praise the Lord from the earth,
Sea monsters and all deeps;
Fire and hail, snow and clouds;
Stormy wind, fulfilling His word;
Mountains and all hills;
Fruit trees and all cedars;
Beasts and all cattle;
Creeping things and winged fowl;
Kings of the earth and all peoples;
Princes and all judges of the earth;
Both young men and virgins;
Old men and children.

Let them praise the Lord,
For His name alone is exalted;
His glory is above earth and heaven.

And He has lifted up a horn for His people,
Praise for all His godly ones;
Even for the sons of Israel, a people near to Him,
Praise the Lord!

Psalm 148

The beasts of the field will glorify Me;
The jackals and the ostriches;
Because I have given waters in the wilderness
And rivers in the desert,
To give drink to My chosen people.

Isaiah 43:20

We tend to automatically assume that this is all figurative, that of course aspects of nature cannot literally praise God, that these are simply "anthropomorphisms" (figures of speech attributing human characteristics or behaviors to things that are not human). What mitigates against this assumption is, first of all, that the Psalmist uses exactly the same language to describe the praise of "…angels…hosts…kings…princes…judges… young men and virgins; old men and children," as He uses to describe that of "…sun and moon…snow and clouds…fruit trees…beasts," etc. He draws no distinction between the two. In fact, verse 13 of Psalm 148 says, "Let **them** praise the Lord" (emphasis added). The pronoun, "them," refers simultaneously to people and objects of nature. This suggests that nature is not being figuratively compared with humans; rather, both are being exhorted to perform the same action. If we take the praise of nature in this Psalm to be figurative, it follows that the praise of humans should be regarded as figurative as well — which it clearly is not!

Secondly, humans and nature are both being told to praise God. It is one thing to merely say that nature praises God; it is another thing to bid it to do so. It would seem exceptionally odd to admonish one to carry out an action that is only figurative.

Thirdly, when Isaiah says, "The beasts of the field will glorify [in the Hebrew, *cabad*, 'honor'] Me," he notes that they have a rationale for this: "...**because** I have given waters in the wilderness and rivers in the desert, to give drink to My chosen people" (emphasis added). If the honoring is only figurative, then is the animals' reason for doing this also figurative? Again, clearly not! Isaiah is saying that the beasts are able to honor God in response to specific blessings. Interestingly, the chosen people's response to these blessings was quite the opposite: "Yet you have not called on me, O Jacob" (verse 22). Sometimes animals are more honoring toward God than humans are!

This raises questions: *how* can aspects of nature praise God? In fact, how can they offer *any* response toward Him? In order to do that, don't they have to be able to think, feel or respond? It is easy to substantiate that with animals. Anyone who has petted a dog or cat has seen it respond joyfully with a wagging tail or an affectionate rub. With regard to us humans, Scripture says that not only our minds, but our spirits are capable of thinking: "For who among men knows the thoughts of a man except the spirit of the man which is in him?" (1 Corinthians 2:11). Contrary to popular thought, animals, too, have spirits: "Who knows if the spirit of man rises upward and if the **spirit** (in Hebrew, *ruach*) **of the animal** goes down into the earth?" (Ecclesiastes 3:21, NIV, emphasis added). If not only their brains, but their spirits, can perceive and think, this might further help to explain how they can respond with praise.

But by what means can the sun, clouds and fruit trees give praise, without the use of a brain? Do plants have personal spirits? Scripture doesn't affirm this, and historically the witness of the church is against this idea. Do inanimate objects have spirits, as Animists believe? Not only does Scripture offer no support for this, but it would seem silly to think that each cloud that forms and disperses within minutes has its own permanent personal spirit.

But this does not mean that the inanimate creation is without spirit and life. Scripture clearly states that God's Spirit is *in* His creation. This is not pantheism — which teaches that God *is* the creation and the creation is God. Rather, it is the time-honored Judeo-Christian belief that God *inhabits* all of His creation. Psalm 139:7 asks, "Where can I go from Your Spirit? Or where can I flee from Your presence?" The answer? Nowhere, because His presence is found throughout creation. Jeremiah 23:24 says, "'Can a man hide himself in secret places so that I cannot see him?' says the Lord. **'Do I not fill the heavens and the earth?'** declares the Lord" (emphasis added).

If the Spirit of God inhabits His creation, does He directly animate it to praise Him, or does He somehow impart to it its own ability to actively respond to Him without the aid of either a brain or a personal spirit? And exactly *how* does it praise Him? Apparently God hasn't deemed it necessary for us to know one way or the other. During the first millennium and beyond, Christians were just fine with that. For instance, in the early sixth century, St. Zosima said, "The whole creation and every creature, every leaflet yearns toward the Word, praises God, mourns before Christ, and achieves this unconsciously through the **mystery** of its blameless life…We alone are the godless and the stupid" (emphasis added).[23] Although Zosima affirmed that nature praises God, he called it a "mystery."

In the late thirteenth century, Thomas of Celano recorded that St. Francis (early thirteenth century)…

> …invited [flowers] to praise the Lord **as though** they were endowed with reason…[and] …exhorted…cornfields and vineyards, stones and forests, and all the beautiful things of the fields, fountains of water and all the green things of the gardens, earth and fire, air and wind, to love God and serve Him (emphasis added).[24]

Notice the words, "as though." Francis did not claim that inanimate nature possessed logic or a will that could *initiate*; only that it could *respond* to God by praising Him in some rudimentary and unknown way.

Hosea confirms this:

> "It will come about in that day that I will respond," declares the Lord. "I will respond to the heavens, and **they will respond** to the earth. And **the earth will respond** to the grain, to the new wine and to the oil, and **they will respond** to Jezreel" (Hosea 2:21-22, emphasis added).

[23] Arseniev, Nicholas, *Mysticism and the Eastern Church* (Crestwood, NY: St. Vladimir's Seminary Press, 1979), 118-119.

[24] Jacobs, Bill, "My Brothers, Birds, You should Praise Your Creator," *Blessed Kateri Tekakwitha Conservation Center*, http://www.conservation.catholic.org, /st_francis_of_ assisi.htm, 2000-2012 (accessed January 2, 2012).

In Hebrew, "respond," *anah*, means to answer, testify or declare. In some cases *anah* means to answer by singing or chanting to each other responsively, as when the people chanted, "Amen," each time the Levites chanted declarations between Mt's Gerazim and Ebal (Deuteronomy 27:14-15), or when the people chanted, "Amen! Amen!" to Ezra's reading of the law (Nehemiah 8:6). Since God and nature both "respond" in Hosea 2:21-22, it has been suggested that this, too, may be responsive chanting, as if nature is saying, "Amen," to God's declarations![25] Until Francis' day, theologians never tried to explain the mechanics of how this works. They were satisfied to leave it a mystery. So will we.

This much we do know: what we do to nature directly reflects our attitude toward our God who created and inhabits it.

To show disrespect toward a gift is to disrespect the giver. How much more so when the Giver's very Spirit infuses that gift! We must treat nature with the utmost reverence, dignity and respect.

In few places do we see life revealed in inanimate nature more pointedly than during Christ's triumphant entry into Jerusalem. Jesus' disciples had joined with the multitude who were praising Him on Palm Sunday. All were crying out, "Blessed is the King who comes in the name of the Lord; Peace in heaven and glory in the highest!" (Luke 19:38). The

---

[25] Uitenbogaard, Arie, "Meaning and Etymology of the Hebrew Name, Anah," *Abarim Publications*, http://www.abarim-publications.com/Meaning/Anah.html#TzlQicWJcmY (accessed February 17, 2012).

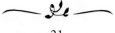

Healing The Earth

Pharisees demanded that Jesus rebuke His disciples. But the Lord responded, "I tell you, if these become silent, the stones will cry out" (Luke 19:40)! Again, is this merely figurative? If the stones would not, in fact, cry out, then what would they do? Just lie there and, in some merely poetic way, bear silent witness? Is that the rebuttal that would have stopped the mouths of the Pharisees? Hardly! Perhaps, in our own celebration of our Lord's eternal Kingdom, we may miss what our Lord actually said here, that in some mysterious and unexplained way God can enable inanimate objects of creation — the stones — to "recognize" who He is and "celebrate" with mankind.

Much of the Lord's Body honors the Apocrypha as part of the Bible. Other portions do not recognize it as canonical (part of Scripture), and some fear it, out of ignorance, as though it were evilly inspired. Most Protestant scholars view it as rich in wisdom but not canonical. Whichever view people hold may be irrelevant here. The reason I share the following from "The Prayer of Azariah and the Song of the Three Young Men" is not to proof-text, as one would from the Bible. I quote excerpts from this beautiful passage to reveal more about how the people of Bible times thought and felt about nature, and what they thought the creation and its creatures were capable of doing — and should do.

Here is some Bible background for "The Prayer of Azariah": King Nebuchadnezzar had decreed "...that at the moment you hear the sound of the horn, flute, lyre, trigon, psaltery, bagpipe, and all kinds of music, you are to fall down and worship the golden image" (Daniel 3:5). Daniel's three young friends refused. Therefore, they were bound and thrown into the fiery furnace, stoked "...seven times more than it was usually heated" (vs. 19). But Nebuchadnezzar was astounded to see "...four men loosed and walking about in the midst of the fire without harm, and the appearance of the fourth is like a son of the gods" (vs. 25). Nebuchadnezzar had been given grace to see what many believe to be an epiphany of the pre-incarnate Christ! According to the Apocrypha, at that time Azariah led his two companions in the following litany of praise (for the sake of brevity we have omitted the refrain after the first few lines). The "Song of Azariah" begins with repentance for the sins of Israel and a plea that God will let their enemies know He is the only God. We begin with vs. 28:

Then the three, as with one mouth, praised and glorified
and blessed God in the furnace, saying:
"Blessed art Thou, O Lord, God of our fathers,
and to be praised and highly exalted forever;
And blessed is Thy glorious, holy name
and to be highly praised and highly exalted forever;
Blessed art Thou in the temple of Thy holy glory,
and to be praised and highly exalted forever.
Blessed art Thou who sittest upon cherubim
and lookest upon the deeps,
and to be praised and highly exalted forever.
Blessed art Thou upon the throne of Thy kingdom
and to be extolled and highly exalted forever.
Blessed art Thou in the firmament of heaven
and to be sung and glorified forever.
Bless the Lord, all works of the Lord,

Healing The Earth

sing praise to Him and highly exalt Him forever.
Bless the Lord, you heavens,
sing praise to Him and highly exalt Him forever.
...Bless the Lord, you angels of the Lord.
...Bless the Lord, all waters above the heaven.
...Bless the Lord, all powers.
...Bless the Lord, sun and moon.
...Bless the Lord, stars of heaven.
...Bless the Lord, all rain and dew.
...Bless the Lord, all winds.
...Bless the Lord, fire and heat.
...Bless the Lord, winter cold and summer heat.
...Bless the Lord, dews and snows.
...Bless the Lord, nights and days.
...Bless the Lord, light and darkness.
...Bless the Lord, ice and cold.
...Bless the Lord, frosts and snows.
...Bless the Lord, lightnings and clouds.
...Let the earth bless the Lord;
Let it sing praise to Him and highly exalt Him forever.
...Bless the Lord, mountains and hills.
...Bless the Lord, all things that grow on the earth.
...Bless the Lord, you springs.
...Bless the Lord, seas and rivers.
...Bless the Lord, you whales and all creatures
  that move in the waters.
...Bless the Lord, all birds of the air.
...Bless the Lord, all beasts and cattle.
[The song concludes with exhortations to men, Israel,

24

priests, servants, spirits of the righteous and all the humble of heart and various other individuals to give thanks to the Lord, for He has rescued them from the hand of death.]

Here are some observations for our hearts and minds. Note the comprehensiveness: Azariah led in prayer for every living creature and every thing in heaven and earth, as if all could somehow "hear" and obey. He exhorted birds of the air, fish, animals and even such inanimate things as winds and snow — to praise the Lord. How often do we pray for animals, much less things, exhorting them to praise the Lord? Or do we at all?

Remember that Psalm 148, quoted earlier, expressed a call for nature to worship God and highly exalt Him forever, in almost identical words. And note that just as in that Psalm, Azariah makes no distinction between humans and nature in their ability to praise God.

Apparently, believers in biblical days thought that all of nature, animate or inanimate, was in some unexplained way able to "recognize" and worship its Creator.

Nature Can Communicate

We quoted Psalm 19:1a. Now, let's look at the next verses (1b-4a):

And their expanse is declaring the work of His hands.
Day to day pours forth speech,

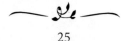

And night to night reveals knowledge.
There is no speech, nor are there words;
Their voice is not heard.
Their line has gone out through all the earth,
And their utterances to the end of the world.

Could this be more than poetic language?

Job counseled his critics to listen to the earth, for the earth would teach them (Job 12:7-8):

But now ask the beasts, and let them teach you;
And the birds of the heavens, and let them tell you.
Or speak to the earth, and let it teach you;
And let the fish of the sea declare to you.

In later chapters, I (John) will testify of some who have indeed learned how to listen to nature. Suffice it here to say that this is not merely figurative speech, for Job went on to say in verse nine, "Who among all these [that is, the beasts, the birds, the earth and the fish] does not know that the hand of the Lord has done this" (that is, afflicted Job)? In verse seven, Job had admonished his three human friends to let all of these "teach" them, inferring that in contrast to these, they did **not** know that the hand of the Lord had done this (at least not in the same way Job meant. They saw Job's afflictions as God's retribution for sins; he saw them as arbitrary acts of God). If Job meant that nature only figuratively knew that the hand of the Lord had done this, the contrast breaks down, unless he meant that his friends were likewise only figuratively ignorant. As a man of faith in his

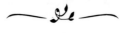

day, Job really believed nature could communicate truth to our hearts and that nature is often more sensitive to the plight of our fellow humans than we are.

The story of Balaam's donkey is even more telling (Numbers 22:1-35). Balak pleaded with Balaam to curse Israel. At first, Balaam refused, saying he could not curse what God had blessed. But Balak sent more envoys, beseeching him, offering him riches and honor. Balaam inquired of the Lord, Who told him to go with them, but to speak only what He had put in his mouth. On the way, Balaam's heart became enticed by offers of wealth (Jude 11), and the Lord was angry with him. God sent an angel to kill him. We pick up the story at that point (vs. 22):

> *But God was angry because he was going, and the angel of the Lord took his stand in the way as an adversary against him. Now he was riding on his donkey and his two servants were with him.*
>
> *When the donkey saw the angel of the Lord standing in the way with his drawn sword in his hand, the donkey turned off from the way and went into the field; but Balaam struck the donkey to turn her back into the way.*
>
> *Then the angel of the Lord stood in a narrow path of the vineyards, with a wall on this side and a wall on that side.*
>
> *When the donkey saw the angel of the Lord, she pressed herself to the wall and pressed Balaam's foot against the wall, so he struck her again.*

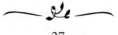

Healing The Earth

The angel of the Lord went further, and stood in a narrow place where there was no way to turn to the right hand or the left.

When the donkey saw the angel of the Lord, she lay down under Balaam; so Balaam was angry and struck the donkey with his stick.

And the Lord opened the mouth of the donkey, and she said to Balaam, "What have I done to you, that you have struck me these three times?"
Then Balaam said to the donkey, "Because you have made a mockery of me! If there had been a sword in my hand, I would have killed you by now!'"

The donkey said to Balaam, "Am I not your donkey on which you have ridden all your life to this day? Have I ever been accustomed to do so?" And he answered, "No."

Then the Lord opened the eyes of Balaam, and he saw the angel of the Lord standing in the way with his drawn sword in his hand; and he bowed all the way to the ground.

The angel of the Lord said to him, "Why have you struck your donkey these three times Behold, I have come out as an adversary, because your way was contrary to me.

But the donkey saw me and turned aside from me these

three times. If she had not turned aside from me, I would surely have killed you just now, and let her live."

And Balaam said to the angel of the Lord, "I have sinned, for I did not know that you were standing in the way against me. Now, if it is displeasing to you, I will turn back."

But the angel of the Lord said to Balaam, "Go with the men, but you shall speak only the word which I shall tell you." So Balaam went along with the leaders of Balak.

What a wondrous story!
Note:
1) The donkey could see God's angel; but Balaam, the Lord's prophet, could not.
2) The Bible does not say that God spoke through the donkey like a hand in a sock puppet. Only demons do that sort of thing. Nor does it say that the donkey merely relayed words dictated directly from God, for she phrased her words to convey her own personal point of view. Rather, it says that God "…opened her mouth" to speak (vs. 28). It was the donkey who spoke.
3) She could reason, and she made a good defense of herself.
4) She could count! She reminded Balaam he had struck her "three times"!
5) She exhibited good memory, recalling to Balaam not only that she was his donkey he had "…ridden all your life to this day," but also that she had never before balked against his commands.
6) She could think. She first turned aside, then pressed his foot against a wall so he couldn't go forward to his doom, and then,

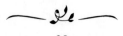

when no other option would save his life, she laid down on the road.

7) She loved unconditionally. She tried three times to save his life, even when he repeatedly struck her!

What was happening here? Could it be that, for the moment, the Lord removed the curse that came upon all animals when Adam and Eve fell? I suspect that before the curse, animals could communicate with far more ease than they do now. Adam and Eve had been created in the image of God; great abilities must have resided naturally in them. When the sinful eating of the tree of knowledge of good and evil occurred under Satan's urging, Adam's and Eve's hearts were filled with Satan's corruption. Because Adam was the head and had named all the animals (which means he determined the destiny for every creature), his corruption now defiled all whose status was below him. If Adam and Eve and all the creatures had retained their original abilities, their corruptions could have wreaked immense havoc! Therefore, God had to turn the power down, not only in Adam and Eve, but in all of His creation. Romans 8:20-21 states this clearly and succinctly: "For the creation was subjected to futility, not of its own will, but because of Him who subjected it, in hope that the creation itself would also be set free from corrupting bondage in order to share the glorious freedom of the children of God."

We know that His hope was for the eventual redemption of mankind and the restoration of all of nature. What happened in this story, I suspect, was that God simply, for that moment, lifted the curse of dumbness from the donkey, restored her to her rightful capabilities, and released her to confront His erring prophet. Through this story, we may be catching a glimpse of the glory of what God created in the animal kingdom.

What the donkey did here may have been normal behavior among all the animals before the Fall.

I am not the first to wonder about this. Throughout Christian and Jewish history there has been witness to this idea. For instance, around the turn of the nineteenth century, St. Seraphim of Sarov, one of the wisest and most prominent Orthodox Christian thinkers of his day, lived in the forests of Russia. He was so kind and filled with the love of God that rabbits, foxes, wolves and other animals would visit with him like tame pets. A bear even ate out of his hand![26] Summing up the wisdom of many Saints throughout the centuries, Seraphim said:

> Owing to the gift of the supernatural grace of God which was infused into Adam by the breath of life, Adam could see and understand the Lord walking in Paradise and comprehend His words and the conversations of the Holy Angels, **and the language of all the beasts, birds, and reptiles,** and all that is now hidden from us fallen and sinful creatures, but was so clear to Adam before the fall (emphasis added).[27]

[26.] Mileant, Bishop Alexander, "St. Seraphim of Sarov Life and Teachings," translated by Nicholas and Natalia Semyanko, *OrthodoxPhotos.com*, http://www.orthodoxphotos.com/readings/SOS/, 2003-2012, (accessed July 7, 2012).

[27.] St. Seraphim of Sarov, *Little Russian Philokalia*, Vol. 1, (Platina, CA: St. Herman of Alaska Press, 1978), 100.

Healing The Earth

According to Josephus Flavius, first century Jews likewise believed that all animals had the power of speech before the Fall.[28] Whether or not this is true (Scripture does not say either way), church history is not without examples much like that of Balaam's donkey. The following are just two of them. Some Christians dismiss such stories as legends or embellished accounts; others accept them as truly historical. Whatever the case may be, these stories exemplify principles that many Christians have believed for many centuries.

It is said that when Artemon of Laodecia, (early 4th century), was arrested for smashing pagan idols, he ordered his entourage of six donkeys and two deer to report his arrest to the bishop. Off they all went, and one of the does delivered the report in a human voice! While Artemon was being tortured on a skewer over a fire, the doe returned and comforted him by licking his burns, then escaped when shot at with arrows. The torturer prepared a cauldron of boiling pitch for Artemon. The doe returned again to warn him: "Know, impious one, that two big birds will grab you and will drop you in the boiler!" A little while later, while the torturer was looking into the cauldron to see if the pitch was boiling, two eagles pulled him off his horse and dropped him in.[29]

A government official named Zoticus (early 4th century) asked for money to buy gems and pearls for the Byzantine emperor, but spent it on caring for lepers. Later, when Constantius, an Arian heretic, took the throne, Zoticus' enemies

---

[28] Josephus, Flavius, *The Works of Josephus*, translated by William Whiston (Peabody, MA: Hendrickson Publishers, 1989), 26.

[29] "Hieromartyr Artemon the Presbyter of Laodicea in Syria," *Orthodox Church in America*, http://ocafs.oca.org/FeastSaintsLife.asp?FSID=101072 (accessed July 16, 2012).

denounced him, claiming that he held subversive beliefs and had misappropriated the emperor's money. In his own defense, Zoticus offered to reveal to Constantius the "gems" and "pearls" he had purchased. When Constantius saw lepers coming to greet him, Zoticus said, "These are the precious stones and brilliant pearls that give luster to the crown of the heavenly Kingdom that you will inherit by their prayers." Infuriated, the Emperor had Zoticus tied behind wild mules and dragged down a hill to his death. Then the mules dragged the body right back up to the summit and proclaimed in a human voice that the martyr must be buried there! Constantius repented, ordered that Zoticus be buried with honor, and decreed that a hospital for lepers be built there, staffed with the finest physicians and caretakers.[30]

If these stories are true, could it be that these animals momentarily regained abilities lost before the fall? Or instead, could it be that Adam understood the animals' own languages, as St. Seraphim seemed to imply in the quote I shared earlier: "Adam could...comprehend...the language of all the beasts, birds, and reptiles." Science is proving that some higher animals do indeed have their own language. Studies of dolphins have revealed that they greet each other by name[31] and announce their names to communicate where they are,[32] in a way that

---

[30] "Martyr Zoticus of Constantinople, Feeder of Orphans (4th c.)," *holytrinityorthodox.com*, http://www.holytrinityorthodox.com/calendar/los/December/31-04.htm (accessed July 16, 2012).

[31] "Dolphin Sounds and Acoustics," *Dolphin Facts and Information*, http://www.dolphins-world.com/Dolphins_Sounds_and_Acoustics.html, 2012 (accessed Jan. 31, 2013).

[32] "Dolphins Identify Themselves with Names," *Softpedia*, http://news.softpedia.com/news/Dolphins-Identify-Themselves-with-Names-23078.shtml, 2001-2013 (accessed Jan. 31, 2013).

expresses mood and motivation[33] ("I'm lost and feeling afraid, and I am trying to find my family"). Researchers have found that their "vocabulary" of calls numbers in the hundreds,[34] and have found evidence that suggests that their dialects (or perhaps even separate languages) may vary from region to region.[35]

Anatomists have discovered that whales, whose squeaky calls have long been known to convey meanings, have "spindle cells" in their brains — cells that until recently were thought to be found only in humans. These cells enable social organization, empathy, intuition about others' feelings, "gut" reactions" and… *speech*. Surprisingly, the brains of whales have three times as many of these cells as do the brains of humans!

Perhaps the most startling discoveries about animal speech have come from studies of prairie dogs in the southwestern U.S., carried out by Dr. Constantine Slobodchikoff, Professor Emeritus at Northern Arizona University. For several decades he has studied their yips, barks and chirps, and has begun to identify the rules of prairie dog grammar in what is proving to be a complex language. Prairie dogs can tell each other who their calls are intended for, whether danger is imminent and what the appropriate response might be.[36] They can communicate whether an intruder is a coyote, domestic dog, human, etc. and

[33.] Yong, Ed, "When Meeting up at Sea, Bottlenose Dolphins Exchange Names-Like Whistles," *Discover, The Magazine of Science, Technology and the Future,* http://blogs. discovermagazine.com/notrocketscience/2012/02/28/when-meeting-up-at-sea-bottlenose-dolphins-exchange-name-like-whistles/#.UQwfUx1X2pY, 2012 (accessed Jan. 31, 2013).

[34.] "Dolphins Identify Themselves with Names," *Softpedia,* http://news.softpedia.com/news/Dolphins-Identify-Themselves-with-Names-23078.shtml, 2001-2013 (accessed Jan. 31, 2013).

[35.] "Dolphin Sounds and Acoustics," *Dolphin Facts and Information,* http://www.dolphins-world.com/Dolphins_Sounds_and_Acoustics.html, 2012 (accessed Jan. 31, 2013).

[36.] Demello, Margo, "Yips, Barks and Chirps, The Language of Prairie Dogs," *Petroglyphs,* http://www.petroglyphsnm.org/wildsides/pdlanguage.html, 2007 (accessed Feb. 1, 2013).

can even tell its size, shape and color,[37] as well as how quickly it is approaching. Prairie dogs have even identified the difference between a tall human in a blue shirt and a short human in a yellow shirt, and talked to each other about them[38] — even when those humans were not present! They can even invent new words to describe new objects or experiences, and teach them to each other, expanding a shared vocabulary![39]

Science aside, since there is no biblical proof that all animals could once talk, or that they will in the new Earth, I will not present speculative theology as if it is an established doctrine. I will leave it in the realm of speculation, where it belongs. And even if this speculation proves true, it goes without saying that few Christians will ever witness events as rare as animals talking. But the stories of Saints Artemon and Zoticus are exceptional examples of two broader principles that should not be considered exceptional…

…that in various ways, animals (and all of nature) can reflect the Glory of God to a greater degree than they do now, when in the presence of loving, righteous Christians whose repentant and holy lifestyles likewise reflect His Glory…and that we too might reflect the glory of God to a greater degree if, in honor of our Maker, we would recognize the magnificence with which He has invested His creatures, and cherish and protect this blessed gift.

---

[37] Wochoven, Natalie, "How Long Until We Learn Animal Languages?" *BETA News*, http://www.petroglyphsnm.org/wildsides/pdlanguage.html, 2012 (accessed Feb. 1, 2013).
[38] "The Tales of the Prairie Dog," *Now I Know*, http://nowiknow.com/the-tales-of-the-prairie-dog/, 2012 (accessed Feb. 1, 2013).
[39] Demello, Margo, (accessed Feb. 1, 2013).

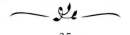

If we did, it would certainly change the way we relate to our fellow creatures. For instance, around the outskirts of some cities in the American west, prairie dog towns are being cleared away for new housing developments. Imagine working on such a project. Would it occur to you to trap prairie dogs and release them in a place safer for them? If you were not able to do this, would it at least occur to you to pray that God help them scamper to a safer place? Would you even feel anything at all for them? Or would you feel no more than you would for the displacement of rocks and dirt?

Their Own Kind of Responsiveness, Feeling and Desire

Ever since Aristotle said that whatever does not breathe or move has no life in it, western culture has increasingly departed from what the Bible says about nature. We have therefore thought that whatever is inanimate is without spirit, feeling, or desire. Objects have become mere lifeless "things" to us, nothing else. But that has never been what God's Word has maintained. Are we willing to let the Lord take us on a walk to Emmaus, as He did with Cleopas and the other disciple, revealing what was always written in His Word, though we didn't see it (Luke 24:13-35)? Listen again to Romans 8:18-22:

> For I consider that the sufferings of this present time are not worthy to be compared with the glory that is to be revealed to us. For the **anxious longing of the creation waits eagerly** for the revealing of the sons of God. For

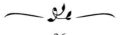

the creation was subjected to futility, not of its own will, but because of Him who subjected it, in hope that the creation itself also will be set free from its slavery to corruption into the freedom of the glory of the children of God. For we know that **the whole creation groans and suffers the pains of childbirth** *together until now.* (emphases added)

Verse 24 goes on to say that we, too, "groan" and "wait eagerly." This passage uses the same Greek words (*stenazo* —"groan," and *ekdechomai* —"eagerly") of both nature and humans. On the one hand, the image of childbirth is figurative; we are not literally coming down nature's birth canal. But what is this figurative of? Real anguish! Real care! Just like us, the creation "...waits eagerly, with anxious longing!" *Stenazo*, "groan," means an inward, unexpressed feeling of sorrow.[40] That is emotion and yearning, not inanimate deadness. That is hope and desire, not inert incapability. Truly, Aristotle's philosophy has been allowed to do us great disservice.

New Agers and occultists have taken (and perverted) territory we Christians should long ago have occupied. New Agers speak of "mother earth," and name her "Gaia." Therefore many Christians fear to embrace too literal an interpretation of verse 22, which says that "...the whole creation **groans** and **suffers** the pains of childbirth" (emphasis added). Let me assure you that we do not believe that the earth is our mother, as New Agers believe. In Galatians 4:19 (NIV), Paul says that he is "...again in the pains of childbirth until Christ is formed

---

[40] Vine, W. E., M.A., *Vine's Expository Dictionary of New Testament Words*, (Iowa Falls, IA: Riverside Book and Bible House, 1940), 518.

in you." No one would maintain that Paul is our mother! That was merely an expression of extreme effort. Rather, nature has strong desire, and is in some unexplained way striving for our benefit. Have we been blind to this? Embracing this will require a revolutionary reversal of our erroneous philosophical and theological paradigms if we are to become consonant with God's Word. At present, we cannot comprehend the fullness of what that means, but shame on us for shying away from even beginning to. For too long we have been held captive to philosophy rather than assenting to the simple message of God's Word (Colossians 2:8).

In *Animals and Man: a State of Blessedness*, Dr. Joanne Stefanatos, a prominent Orthodox Christian veterinarian, expresses the same faith that all of nature is an expression of God's glory:

> Blessedness was the original state of existence of Adam and Eve in the Garden of Eden, **and of all the animals before the fall**. Blessedness in God is the ultimate aim of man's existence on earth. God created man as the crown of earthly creation, as the "image of God" in the world by word and deed. **Man, by linking the material creation with the spiritual, can bring down upon earth blessings from heaven and unite all things of earth with God, and maintain all creatures in a state of love, harmony and order** (emphases added).[41]

[41.] Stefanatos, Joanne, D.V.M., *Animals and Man: A State of Blessedness*, (Minneapolis, MN: Light and Life Publishing Co., 1992), 11.

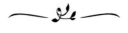

Later, she quotes St. Maximos, a seventh century theologian, who encapsulated the thinking of the early church up until his day:

> Man is not a being isolated from the rest of creation; by his very nature he is bound up with the whole of the universe... In his way to union with God, man in no way leaves creatures aside, but gathers together in his love the whole cosmos disordered by sin, that it may be transfigured by grace.[42]

Dr. Stefanatos' and St. Maximos' statements express well the theme and purpose of this book. To whatever degree God enables us this side of His second coming, we are to release the creation from its bondage to decay and transform it to become again the expression, with us, of the intent of God that all that He made should more fully reveal the glory of His nature.

---

[42] Stefanatos, 76.

CHAPTER THREE

TESTIMONIES AND TEACHINGS, REPENTANCES AND RECONCILIATIONS

Just as the Kingdom of God among men comes by transforming each person one-by-one, at least in some cases restoring the Kingdom among animals arrives the same way. We need to learn how to pray for the healing of the hearts and spirits of animals. Animals have memories, as we saw in Numbers 22. Balaam's ass could remember her life's service to him, and could recall his erring mind to that fact (vs. 30). As we mentioned in the previous chapter, animals have spirits: "Who knows if the spirit of man rises upward and the **spirit of the animal** goes down into the earth?" (Ecclesiastes 3:21, NIV, emphasis added). Having memories and spirits, they can be blessed and retain healthy patterns of reaction, but they can also be wounded and retain hurtful reactions. Any pet owner can attest to the fact that when pets are trained through kindly treatment to respond to affection, they give love in return. But consider how defensive and even cruel an abused pet can become. Animals can be conditioned to be hurtful — or loving.

Sometimes animals may be healed simply by being removed from unkind or vicious treatment and placed in loving homes. Often, a cringing animal has been turned into an affectionate friend. But sometimes the damage has created ingrained patterns too strong to be overcome merely by touches of love.

If we want to heal the wounds of our pets or other animals, we will first need to undergo spiritual hygiene. We know that if we would ascend into the Lord's presence, we must first cleanse our hearts, for, "…Who may ascend the hill of the Lord? And who may stand in His holy place? He who has clean hands and a pure heart" (Psalm 24:3-4a). And we know that if we pray that God will reform parents, brothers and sisters or any other person, God will not hear us if we harbor resentments or judgments against them. So we undertake whatever spiritual disciplines of forgiveness and reconciliation are required.

More than forty years ago, the Lord called me and many others to pioneer in praying for the healing of animals and aspects of His creation. In my case, He ordered me into a discipline for the cleansing of my heart. He directed me to allow His Holy Spirit to recall to my mind, throughout my entire history, every instance of sinful reaction to animals and nature. In His still, small voice, He commanded me to celebrate and give thanks to Him for every positive encounter, and to repent and ask forgiveness for every negative and hurtful reaction. (Many others have now undergone the same discipline.)

For example, I remembered bicycling in Kansas against a fierce gale, hardly making headway, cursing the winds, especially on cold days when the bitter chill pierced through my overcoat. The Holy Spirit called me to repent, lest the next hard wind activate negative expectations and feelings in me.

But the question is, do those emotional reactions in some way actually wound nature? Let me repeat what I said in Chapter Two: we have been raised to think, according to Aristotle, that whatever does not move or breathe has no life or spirit in it. Again, think about Romans 8:19: "For the anxious longing of the creation waits eagerly for the revealing of the sons of God." Paul unabashedly attributed powerful emotions to God's creation.

Job did the same. He told his friends:

> If my **land cries out** against me, and its **furrows weep** together, if I have eaten its fruit without money, or have caused its owners to lose their lives, let briars grow instead of wheat, and stinkweed instead of barley (Job 31:38-40, emphasis added).

In the Hebrew, "cries out," *za'aq*, means "to shriek from anguish or danger."[43] This is a cry of distress; our land is wounded by the way we treat others, and its response is to lose productivity, just as happened when Cain killed his brother,

---

[43] "Job 31:38," *Biblios.com*, http://www.scripturetext.com/job/31-38.htm (accessed July 7, 2012).

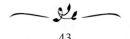

Healing The Earth

Abel:

> *The voice of your brother's blood is crying [in Hebrew, the same word, za'aq] to Me from the ground. Now you are cursed from the ground, which has opened its mouth to receive your brother's blood from your hand. When you cultivate the ground, it will no longer yield its strength to you; you will be a vagrant and a wanderer on the earth* (Genesis 4:10b-12a).

Many Christians today have come to understand this, and celebrate God's present move to change minds and hearts. He wants to open us to better, fuller and more wholesome relationships with nature and its creatures — as He intended from the beginning, before the Fall.

To cleanse my own heart, I repented not only of holding bitterness against cold winds. I repented for any way my reactions might have wounded God's creation. I asked that I be forgiven, and reconciled to winds and cold.

The Lord recalled to my mind the times when my cow, "Spring," swished her poop-laden tail against my face while I was milking her — and the angry reactions I made, as though she had done that on purpose. I repented for my animosities, and asked God's forgiveness. But Spring was a saint. My other cow, "Queenie," was like the devil incarnate! She would rise up on her hind legs and bash down any fence, getting out to plunder the neighbors' gardens and mine. Each time I herded her back into the compound, she would sense just the right moment to veer away from the gate and dash back out to trample my garden.

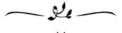

One afternoon, exasperated to the max, I shouted curse words at her at the top of my lungs — and all the neighbors heard words they never knew existed — as did my mother, who called me in and read the Scriptures to me. Later, when undergoing the discipline of reconciling with nature, I repented and asked the Lord to cleanse my heart. I tried to forgive Queenie, but I have to admit that when my parents sold her I rejoiced greatly! How many others can relate stories of exasperation with pets and other animals? The question is, "How many of these have been addressed in prayers of repentance and reconciliation?"

Winters were often so cold I would milk with one hand while warming my fingers between the cow's bag and her leg — while my toes froze right through heavy socks and boots. How I hated the cold! That required even more repentance and reconciliation with the creation. Think back; how often have you reacted in anger and cursing (whether in foul language or merely felt and repressed)? For example, at stinging bursts of sleet hitting your face, or the cold freezing your toes? More importantly, have you made all such experiences objects of healing prayers, either by yourself or by others praying with you?

In the spring, composted manure had to be wheel barrowed out and spread over the surface of my half-acre garden. But it was often muddy, and the wheelbarrow would get stuck or, worse, the wheel would drop into a hidden hole and topple me over it into the muck and manure! My feelings and consequent words ought not to be repeated here — or anywhere! The Lord called me to repent of feelings about muck and manure, "stubborn and stupid" wheelbarrows, and awful smells and sights.

I had to review my entire life, recalling incidents with

— ✑ —

45

animals and other aspects of creation — like freezing cold, wind and sleet in the winter, or the summer sun that burned down on me while streams of sweat sent dirt rivers running down my face as I hoed the weeds out of row after row of corn and beans. I especially had to repent of my attitude toward morning glories. Those weeds propagated by sending roots underground, to pop up randomly all over the garden. No matter how many times I chopped them out, here they would come again, especially in areas I had just weeded yesterday. I hated them with a passion! And the gnats that buzzed about my ears, and the mosquitoes that "delighted" to torment me, as I tried to hoe and swat at the same time. Those were events that called for cleansing of my heart.

How many "morning glories" of bitterness, both little and huge, still crop up in the garden of your life from roots as yet unseen or ferreted out? Or worse, seen but resisting healing prayer? The discipline of purifying the heart often calls for stubbornly insistent prayers!

Crows would land on my corn and peck holes in the ears. I would curse at them while trying to pick them off with my BB gun. Then when we'd have corn on the cob, occasionally we'd crunch our teeth when we bit into a BB! Rabbits would chew up my vegetable plants. Potato bugs would cluster on my potato plants, and require hours of patiently picking them off (if we didn't want to spray poison). All these and more made for hours of prayer, until I could recall no more incidents — only to have the Lord, whose memory of everything we have done never fails, bring up a bunch more! At long last, it seemed my heart and mind were clear, and I could pray effectively for God's creation. Some have testified that it has been so for them. Such a discipline must become thorough in all of us who have been called to minister to nature.

The teaching? Everything we have felt and done has left deposits in us that either bless or wound ourselves, others and the creation. Think about it. Ask the Holy Spirit to persist, revealing and cleansing until finally He says, "Okay, that's enough." Maybe all things don't have to be recalled specifically and directly prayed about, but in my case the Lord didn't seem to be satisfied with general prayers. He kept at it down to the least detail, even such a seemingly innocuous thing as the resentment I nursed after stubbing my toe against a stone.

For me, one good fruit of this discipline is that I am comfortable in all of nature, and I feel very loved and refreshed in the woods. Another is that my garden goes crazy overproducing, and, as Mark mentioned earlier, all the neighbors marvel and ask, "How come ours don't produce that well?" Others have testified to me of their wildly abundant gardens and farmers' fields since they have been praying for the healing of the earth.

Remember what happened when Adam ate the forbidden fruit (Genesis 3:17b, NIV)? "Cursed is the ground because of you; through painful toil you will eat of it all the days of your life." The curse increased when Adam's son, Cain, slew his brother Abel (Genesis 4:11-12): "Now you are cursed from the ground, which has opened its mouth to receive your brother's blood from your hand. When you cultivate the ground, **it will no longer yield its strength to you**" (emphasis added).

Could it be that many who can testify to superabundant gardens, although unaware of the principles I have been sharing,

4

have none the less become so healed in their hearts that nature **will** release its abundance to them? In the "Transformations" video series by George Otis, Jr., it was reported that before the great move of God in Almolonga, Guatemala, plants were spindly and the land produced only one crop per year, but after the people were converted and changed their ways and blessed the earth, it produced three crops a year — with carrots the size of a man's forearm! Nature **will** yield its fruits to us, when our hearts are right.

The fruits of my prayers and those like me have been undeniable blessings.

I write to encourage Christians to plunge with a willing heart into prayers for cleansing and reconciliation regarding each incident in their lives concerning any and every part of nature. This is especially true for those of us who would be used by our loving Lord to heal aspects of creation.

Healing Animals

Once the heart is prepared, we can be used by God to heal His beloved animals. Our son Loren's sister-in-law, Anne, came to live with us for a while, bringing with her a little dog, named "Cheney." Cheney was the worst dog imaginable — disobedient, loud at all times of the day or night and, worst of all, chasing little children who came onto the lawn, nipping at their heels. We became afraid of possible law suits. No corrections or disciplines had any affect. Finally, I said, "I'm either going to kill that dog — or heal it!" So, first

I had to repent and ask God to give me a heart of love for Cheney. I took her on my lap and prayed for her as though she possessed a mind that could understand everything I said. Perhaps in her spirit she could, but whether or not, I knew God could relay the message to her.

Of course, it is always easiest to pray about events in an animal's life that you or someone you know has witnessed first-hand. But one thing that can make praying over animals more difficult is that where there are no witnesses, they can't tell you their hurtful memories. Don't think that you always have to know the memory in order to bring healing. God's healing power is not dependent on knowledge. In some cases, the Holy Spirit might prefer that you simply pray without knowing what abuse or trauma the animal has experienced. But in some cases, God may reveal it in order to give you deeper love and empathy for the animal, and perhaps to increase the joy you feel when healing comes.

How do you know that you have heard correctly? There are times when, after the fact, persons who actually witnessed the abuse or trauma have stepped up to offer confirmation. Where that is not available, dramatic and immediate improvements in the animal's behavior can attest that you were on the right track. Such was the case with Cheney. I asked the Lord to give me words of knowledge (if that was within His will) by which to know what had happened to cause her to be so difficult. What came to me was that, when she was a puppy, little children had teased her viciously, beaten her and chased her. I repented on behalf of the children, and asked God to enable her spirit to forgive them, and to so heal her heart that her behaviors could change.

Healing The Earth

It continually amazes me how quickly and easily animals forgive (that is, if prayed for; I have known animals that were not prayed for who held grudges for years). If only we humans were that humane, what a wonderful world it would be!

Cheney became a wonderful little dog! She welcomed children and played happily around them, quit her loud barking at everything, and became very obedient. Best of all, for those who saw her transformation, she became a testimony of the healing love of God.

She especially loved me. In the mornings, when I would awaken I would look down, there would be Cheney beside the bed, politely waiting for me, asking permission with her eyes. When I would say, "Okay," she would leap onto the bed and happily wash my face! Whenever I sat in my recliner, she would ask permission, and then climb onto my lap, growling happy warnings if anyone seemed to be intending to hurt me.

Our son, John, had a horse farm where he kept "Smoky," a large gelding who had an annoying way of purposely brushing against fences to trap legs and throw riders off. Though he stood more than sixteen hands tall and was strong, he was skittish and fearful like a little colt. I walked up to him, put my arms about his neck, and asked God to allow me to find and heal the roots of his troubled character. The Holy Spirit revealed that, like Cheney, he had been mistreated as a colt. Farmer's children had ridden him with cruel insensitivity. They had whipped him and given him no loving affection. Again I prayed, believing that either his spirit could hear and understand, or at least that God could hear and heal. Smoky changed overnight! What a testimony to God's power he became! Again, it's strange and

wonderful to me that animals can be healed much more quickly and easily than people!

Mrs. Barth, one of my parishioners who lived on a farm, had a small dog who was deathly afraid of children. If a child approached, it would cringe and urinate on the floor. I asked Mrs. Barth if she would allow me to minister to her dog. When she said "Yes," I prayed as I related earlier, asking the Lord to reveal what had happened. As a puppy, she too had been kicked and beaten by senseless farm children. I prayed in the same way, asking God to enable the dog to forgive their meanness. A few days later, I again called on Mrs. Barth with our son, John, who was then about four years old. I had forgotten to tell Johnny about the dog's peculiarity. He ran right to her, hugged her, and romped on the floor with her. She didn't cringe or pee, and enjoyed playing with him. She too became a testimony to God's healing love.

Other Christians have related to me many such stories of the healing and transformation of animals, but they all bear the same stamp — woundings in the animals' earlier life, and negative reactions that persist into the present. I don't know that we need to understand how animals can respond to the prayers we say for them. As I have said, perhaps on some level they do hear and understand what we say. Or maybe it is only that our Lord hears and understands for them, and applies the prayers. There are mysteries beyond our comprehension. My point is that such questions need not deter us. I and others have simply prayed for animals as God has led, and whether or not they actually did comprehend, they were healed.

Some woundings are caused by present traumas and can

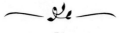

create strong reactions. There had been a sudden storm on my friend's farm. Lightning had struck perilously close to one of his cows. She was so traumatized that she lay down and refused to get up (if a cow does not stand, she will die). The farmer had tried everything to get her to her feet, even twisting her tail and slapping her behind, but nothing had worked. He used his backhoe to carry her into the barn and deposited her beside some hay, hoping she would at least eat and maybe regain enough normalcy to get up. But there she lay, staring catatonically at nothing. The farmer explained to me what had happened, and then he walked off to do some chores, leaving me with the cow. I silently prayed, asking God's permission to minister to her. I knelt in front of her, looked into her eyes, and prayed that God would come to her and heal the trauma from the lightning, casting away her fear by His love. And then I too walked away to be with my friend. When we came back a few minutes later, there she was, standing up, contentedly munching on the hay. The farmer slapped his forehead in surprise and exclaimed, "Holy cow!" That became her name. "Holy Cow" remained good and faithful, delivering a calf every spring and giving milk regularly. And best of all, the farmer was drawn closer to the heart of God.

Countless people can relate similar stories. It's a common practice among many Christians to pray for their pets when they become ill. But it seems to me that, as yet, too few realize that prayer for inner healing, which we have learned to employ for human beings, can be applied to animals. Many have not yet understood that aberrant behaviors in their animals can be transformed by their prayers. Thus, owners have all too often simply suffered whatever distasteful or bothersome behaviors have continued in the pets they love. They have tried, by discipline and love, to effect changes, which have often failed. One of the purposes of this book is to issue a call to learn how to pray to set our animals free into the good behaviors which they, and our loving Lord, really want, and so provide another means through which to draw humans closer to our loving Lord as well.

Prayers for animals, either for simple physical healing or for healing of traumatic wounds, don't need to be much different than those prayed for people. As I said before, I don't know if animals actually understand in their spirits, but I know God hears and answers our prayers. More importantly, I know such prayers are not merely our asking Him to bless something **we** want to do; they are expressions of **His** desire to comfort and heal His creation. God wants more fervently than any of us to heal and restore; it is He who ministers through our prayers. We have only the joy of being instruments in His hands of love.

For humans troubled in heart, we who are prayer counselors have frequently had to interview, counsel and pray over and over, often covering the same ground from several angles, before the person is fully healed. Not so with animals. I have never had to repeat prayers for any animal. They receive and are transformed the first time! Others have testified to the same anointing and success. For me, the Holy Spirit has always revealed the major causative factors in the first application of prayer. But I suppose that akin to humans, there might occasionally be other issues as yet unseen that could require additional prayers. So don't be dismayed if at first your prayers don't seem to succeed. Seek other historical factors that may require healing. "My people are destroyed for lack of knowledge" (Hosea 4:6). The same lack of knowledge may hinder ministry to His creation. Let's keep on, knowing it is God, more than us, Who wants to heal and transform.

Let's respond to God's calling to heal His creation, beginning (as I have said) with whatever animal or aspect of creation He sets before us, until the little corner of His earth that He has entrusted to each of us is truly covered with the knowledge of the Lord, as Isaiah 11:6-9 so wondrously predicts will happen in its fullness when Christ returns:

> *And the wolf will dwell with the lamb,*
> *And the leopard will lie down with the young goat.*
> *And the calf and the young lion and the fatling together;*
> *And a little boy will lead them.*
> *And the cow and the bear will graze.*
> *Their young will lie down together,*
> *And the lion will eat straw like the ox.*
> *The nursing child will play beside the hole of the cobra,*
> *And the weaned child will put his hand on the viper's den.*
> *They will not hurt or destroy in all My holy mountain,*
> *For the earth will be full of the knowledge of the Lord*
> *As the waters cover the sea.*

CHAPTER FOUR

ANIMALS CAN THINK!

The corporate mental stronghold of Aristotelianism has caused many to believe that animals can neither reason nor have spiritual perceptions and responses, that they know nothing and respond solely by instinct or conditioning. In the seventeenth century, Descartes called them "Machines". It was through him (whom many have called "the father of philosophy") that these ideas have become popular today.[44]

But once again, listen to the Scriptures: "The beasts of the field will glorify me, the jackals and the ostriches, because I have given waters in the wilderness" (Isaiah 43:20). Is that ability to glorify God merely instinctual, or does it portray spiritual sensitivity and the ability to think?

Job told his faulty advisors to let nature teach them

---

[44] Hearnshaw, L.S., *Discourse on Method* (New York, NY: Routledge and Kegan Paul, 1987), 69.

wisdom: "But now ask the beasts, and let them teach you; and the birds of the heavens, and let them tell you. Or speak to the earth, and let it teach you; and let the fish of the sea declare to you" (Job 12:7-8). Was that only figurative language, merely a poetic way of speaking?

Can animals think? Doesn't 2 Peter 2:12 call them "unreasoning animals…creatures of instinct?" And doesn't Jude 1:10 say that scoffers "…know by instinct, like unreasoning animals?" It is certainly true that animals lead much of their lives according to instinct, and that their powers of comprehension (even when restored to their condition in Eden) will always be less than ours, for we alone are made in God's image. It goes without saying that even in the new Earth no animal will ever paint a masterpiece or propose a scientific theory. But Peter's and Jude's off-hand remarks are generalized statements, not meant to be taken as comprehensive guides on the matter of animal intellect. For that, we must take into account a fuller array of passages from throughout Scripture, some of which indicate that while animals are largely creatures of instinct, many do possess a remarkable degree of reasoning power (I'll share more from Scripture later).

Science also provides numerous examples. For instance, Jane Goodall observed chimpanzees creating tools made of twigs to ferret out termites. She noted that this was a learned trait, not an instinct. Gorillas and chimps have been taught sign language; one gorilla named "Koko" has acquired a vocabulary of over 1,000 words, and understands spoken English. A bonobo chimp named "Kanzi" has learned to compose short sentences on a symbol board, using 126 characters.[45] In Japan, crows have been seen carefully positioning nuts in front of oncoming cars to get them to crack them open, then waiting for the light to turn red before retrieving their reward — obviously a learned trait![46] In experiments, a Caledonian crow named "Betty" learned to reach with a hooked wire into a container to pull out a bucket of food. She even demonstrated analytical reasoning. To the researchers' astonishment, when another bird stole her wire, she found another straight wire and beat the end into the shape of a hook! And when given a box of tools, she was able to select the correct width and length needed for the task at hand.[47] Animals can feel; elephants and other species grieve for lost loved ones.[48] Animals can be compassionate; who has not heard stories of dolphins that saved people from sharks or from drowning at sea? How was that mere instinct?

Just as some humans are brilliant and others are slow, so it is with animals. Some are more "awake" than others. Some are much more keenly intelligent than others. And some seem to not be smart at all. For instance, there are many birds that care wisely and meticulously for their young. But God says of the ostrich, "She treats her young harshly, as if they were not hers; she cares not that her labor was in vain, **for God did not endow her with wisdom or give her a share of good sense**" (Job 39:16,17, NIV emphasis added). Many friends have commented to me about how this or that pet is extremely

---

[45.] Stefanatos Joanne, D.V.M., *Animals Sanctified*, a *Spiritual Journey* (Minneapolis, MN: Light and Life Publishing Co., 2001), 178-179.
[46.] Attenborough, David, BBC Wildlife, "Wild Crows Inhabiting the City Use it to their Advantage, "video clip, *Youtube*, Feb. 12, 2007 (accessed June 30, 2012).
[47.] Clayton, Nicola and Emory, Nathan, "Corvid Cognition," *Acadamia.edu*, http://qmul.academia.edu/NathanEmery/Papers/226987/Corvid_Cognition, 2012 (accessed July 18, 2012).
[48.] Stefanatos, 180.

intelligent — or, "That animal is so dumb!" A prophetic friend used to tell me, joyfully, how she could commune so easily with many parts of God's creation. I remember, though, how she made me laugh one day when she joked, "I swear, mosquitoes have got to be the dumbest creatures in all of God's creation!" while she swatted and scratched!

But with regard to many of the higher animals, I tell you that they not only think; they can plot a scheme and carry it out. I grew up on a farm and spent my summers on my grandfather's cattle ranch. But when I went riding as an adult, it had been many years since I had been on a horse. Knowing that, a farmer saddled his gentle mare for me. His teenage daughter rode bareback on the mare's colt, a young stallion. Horses observe protocol. The mare was furious that her colt was proceeding in front of her — he should have followed her lead! I knew and understood her feelings. She plotted how to put her young stallion in his place. Suddenly, she dashed ahead up an incline, lashed out behind with her hooves, smiting her colt's chest, and then ran on and swerved suddenly before a huge boulder, trying to dislodge me. Having sensed what she was plotting, I was ready and was not thrown off. The mare knew that incline was ahead, and beyond it, the boulder. She planned and executed her plot expertly! But, if I had not been aware of her scheming...

When Mark was barely two years old and still in diapers, our cat played with him. Seeing how he would run back and forth between the kitchen and the dining room, she invented a game. She hid behind the open door, and when Mark came running out of the kitchen, she sprang out, caught his diaper in her claws, swung her body and let go. Mark plopped onto his bottom! Mark got up and ran back into the kitchen. By then, the cat had anticipated what he would do, and was hiding again behind the door. She sprang out and caught his diaper again, swung herself, let go, and once more Mark plummeted onto his bottom and giggled with delight. Mark had caught onto the game, and the two of them played at it for quite a while. I swear I saw that cat laughing along with Mark each time she plopped him! That could not have been mere instinct. The cat saw what Mark was doing, invented the game, and knew she could anticipate his movements. It took great skill to catch his diaper without clawing him. She was careful not to injure him. She enjoyed the game in harmony with Mark, knowing he was not hurt, and even appeared to be laughing with him, until they both grew tired and quit.

I shared earlier about my cow, Spring. If there's a bovine Heaven, she's in it. But if there's a cow Hell, Queenie is its leading citizen! (I'm only jesting; I don't really know if there are animals in Heaven or Hell. But on the other hand, if there aren't animals in Heaven, how does Jesus come riding out of Heaven on a white horse?) Queenie could plot and carry out more mischief than anyone could have believed she could think of. As I said before, Spring could swish her manure-clogged tail onto my face while I was milking — but I'm sure she didn't do that intentionally; she was just swatting flies. But I'm just as sure Queenie would do it maliciously! Cunningly, she would note when her tail had been dipped in wet manure, so she could swipe it onto my face! No one can tell me she wasn't capable of wily thinking — I was the brunt of it too many times We finally sold her, and I pitied the next owners!

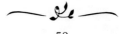

Healing The Earth

My grandfather's ranch hands used to carefully warn us kids about the meanness of some horses. For instance, some could puff up their belly so that, later on, the cinch straps would loosen, slip their saddles, and dump their riders. The ranch hands learned how to drive a knee hard into the horse's side, forcing it to release its pumped-up air. Some horses would dash under a low branch to dislodge an unwary rider. And so on. We learned that some horses could be diabolically clever. On the other hand, good and loving horses would step carefully so as to protect. They can think.

In Chapter Two, I discussed the story of Balaam's donkey. That isn't the only instance in Scripture of animals' ability to think. In 1 Kings, chapter 13, God sent a young prophet from Judah to prophesy to King Jeroboam of Israel that a future king named "Josiah" would remove idolatry from the land. God instructed the prophet to abstain from bread and water until he got back home to Judah, and not to return the way he had come. An old prophet put him to the test. He lied to the young prophet, claiming that an angel had said he must turn back the way he had come, and that he should share a meal with him. After the meal, the young prophet left, and a lion killed him on the road.

Later, the old prophet found the lion standing beside the young prophet's donkey. It had not eaten its prey nor harmed the donkey or anyone passing by. Nor did it harm the old prophet as he laid the young prophet's body on the donkey and removed it from the lion's presence. This lion resisted every instinct; it calculatedly did God's bidding and waited for the old prophet's arrival, so that no one else could remove the body before he could claim it and bury it in his own tomb!

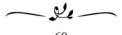

The whale that swallowed Jonah was likewise intelligently responsive to God's call, and sensed exactly the right shore on which to deposit him (Jonah 2:10). Contrary to instinct, in the midst of a drought and famine, ravens resisted eating the bread they had found, and instead brought it to Elisha at the Kerith Ravine (1 Kings17:5-6).

Are the animals in Heaven spoken of in Revelation literal? At least not in all cases. Certainly, Jesus is not literally a lion or a lamb. But what about the eagle who says, "Woe, woe, woe to those who dwell on the earth" (Revelation 8:13)? And what about the "four living creatures?" The Greek word used here for "living creatures" is zoon (pronounced zō-ōn), from which we derive our English word, "Zoo." It means "beast" or "animal." In Revelation 6:1-8, they are reported to announce the arrival of four horses, each carrying a rider. The four horses not only speak; they understand what they are saying, and fall down and worship God (Revelation 5:8). Could these be literal animals? We do not know.

In any case, could it be that animals had such abilities in the garden, and that they will again, in the new Earth? Again, we do not know. But we do know that in this age, we Christians are being "…transformed …from glory to glory" (2 Corinthians 3:18). That process will culminate when we enjoy the fullness of glory in the new Earth, when animals will fulfill much more of their calling than they do now. And in the present world, just as our own process of transformation is a foretaste of our future blessedness, surely animals too may enjoy a foretaste of whatever blessings are to come. The lives of God's saints have always been marked by an ability to relate to animals like Adam

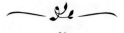

did in paradise. History is brimming with such accounts.

Here are just two stories that reveal how wondrously animals can think and act out a plan, and how their encounters with men of God brought out the best in them (taken from *Animals and Man: a State of Blessedness,* by Joanne Stefanatos).

[Around the turn of the fifth century] there was a man following the anchorite mode [a solitary life of prayer] and rule of life whom two monks of Nitria set out to find. They were, indeed, coming from a distant region, but they had once been the object of his special affection when they lived in a monastery, and they had heard subsequently of his miracles. After a long and intensive search, they finally found him in the seventh month, living on the very edge of the desert, near Memphis. It was said he had been inhabiting those solitudes for twelve years. In spite of his desire to avoid any meeting with man, he did not flee from the visitors when he recognized them. He even devoted himself for three days to their friendly demands. On the fourth day, when they left, he went forward a short distance to accompany them. Suddenly, they saw a lioness of remarkable size coming toward them. The beast, although confronted with three men, had no hesitation as to which she would approach. She lay down at the feet of the anchorite. Lying there, she whimpered and whined and gave signs of grieving and at the same time of asking for something. All three men were moved, especially the anchorite, since the request was directed to him. The lioness went ahead and they followed. She

stopped from time to time, and from time to time looked back, making it clear that what she wanted was that the anchorite should follow where she was leading. Why lengthen the tale? They came to the beast's cave. Here the unfortunate mother nourished five cubs now well-grown, who were born with closed eyes and had been blind ever since. One by one the mother brought them from the cave and laid them at the feet of the anchorite. At last, the Saint saw what the beast was asking for. He called on God's name and with his hands touched the closed eyes of the cubs. At once, the darkness was dispelled, the beasts' eyes were opened, and the light long denied them shone in. This done, the brothers returned. They had visited the anchorite they were eager to see and had received a very rich reward for their toil. They had become witnesses of a great miracle. As well as the Saint's faith, they had seen Christ's glory, to which they were called to testify. The story embraces still another miracle. After five days, the lioness returned to her benefactor, bringing him as a gift the skin of a rare animal. The Saint would frequently wear this as a mantle, not declining to receive from the beast a gift he believed to have quite another source.[49]

What a story! Observe that the lioness knew she needed special help for her cubs. She knew the saint and where he lived, and sensed that he could help her cubs. She approached him with sensitivity and humility, careful not to frighten the men

[49] Stefanatos, Joanne, D.V.M., *Animals and Man: A State of Blessedness* (Minneapolis, MN: Light and Life Publishing Co., 1992), 109-111.

away. She very well communicated her need for help. She led the three carefully, pausing to make sure they were following. She knew better than to invite the men to come into her lair, which might have been too frightening and too dark for them, so she brought out her cubs one by one and laid them at the feet of the Saint. Perhaps just as marvelously, she knew to express her gratitude with a gift, selecting with care a rare animal's skin which she brought to him.

Another example (from the same book):

We saw another man equally remarkable. He lived in a tiny hut not big enough for more than one. It was told of him that a she-wolf regularly attended him at dinner. The beast almost never failed to come running up at the regular mealtime. She would wait outside the door until the hermit would hand out whatever bread was left over from his meal. She would lick his hand and, as if having performed the proper courtesies and extended her greetings, would go away.

It once happened that the holy man had a brother visit him and was accompanying him on his way home. In consequence, he was away some little while and failed to return until nightfall. Meanwhile the beast presented herself at the customary mealtime. She sensed that the cell was empty and that her familiar patron was not at home. She went in, making a careful search where the master could be. By chance, a palm-leaf basket hung nearby, containing five loaves of bread. The wolf took one

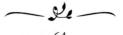

of these and devoured it. After perpetrating this crime, she went away. On his return, the hermit saw that the basket was disarranged and did not contain the proper number of loaves. He realized there had been a theft from his supply, and near the threshold found fragments of the loaf that had been eaten. He then had no uncertainty about the identity of the thief. In the following days, the beast did not come as usual. She was, no doubt, conscious of her presumptuous deed and was refraining from visiting the victim of her wrong-doing. On his part, the hermit was distressed at losing the comfort of the guest and companion of his meals. After seven days, recalled by the hermit's prayers, the wolf was there again, as before, for dinner. The embarrassment of the penitent was easy to see. The wolf did not presume to come close. In deep shame, she would not lift her eyes from the ground. It was plain that she was imploring some act of pardon. The hermit had pity on her confusion. He ordered her to come near, and with a caressing hand stroked her head. Then he refreshed the culprit with a double ration of bread. The wolf received her pardon. She put her grief aside and renewed her habitual visits.[50]

Mark the behavior of the she-wolf, and her intelligence. As many tame animals can do, she could keep a schedule, appearing regularly at the same time. She knew she had done wrong, and had a real conscience and consequent guilt.

[50.] Stefanatos, Joanne, D.V.M., *Animals and Man: A State of Blessedness* (Minneapolis, MN: Light and Life Publishing Co., 1992), 108-109.

She stayed away because of that. When summoned, she demonstrated repentance and humility. She read well the heart of the hermit, and knew she had been forgiven. Her behavior was more humane than many humans manifest!

Interestingly, just as we completed this book, Mark ran across a story that appeared on MSNBC about a group of lions whose behavior was likewise more humane and intelligent than many humans. In Ethiopia, seven men captured a twelve-year-old girl and beat her in an effort to force her to marry one of them. Three lions chased them away and protected her until police and relatives arrived, after which the lions relinquished her and sauntered away into the forest. Locals called this a miracle, but a wildlife expert could find no place for that in his worldview. He speculated instead that the lions might have mistaken the girl's whimpers for the mewing of a lion cub.[51] What he did not explain was why all three lions — whose eyesight is five times as acute as that of humans — were too far-sighted to tell the difference from a distance of a few feet! Nor did he explain why, with their superb sense of smell, they were not tempted by the blood that oozed from cuts left by her beatings — for the entire half day they guarded her! Nor did he explain why they so gladly released their "cub" to a gang of humans — after they had rescued her from another gang of humans that had tormented her so savagely!

It is far more plausible that the lions were savvy enough to tell which humans were safe for the girl and which were not. But among us humans, even an "expert" didn't have enough savvy

[51.] "Ethiopian Girl Reportedly Guarded by Lions," *Associated Press*, June 21, 2005, http://www.msnbc.msn.com/id/8305836/ns/world_news-africa/t/ethiopian-girl-reportedly-guarded lons/#.TyA1_aWJcmY (accessed Jan. 24, 2012).

to recognize the lions' savvy. What lengths we will go to in order to remain safe within our paradigms! Any rationalizing will do, no matter how absurd.

I could share dozens more stories of animals' intelligence and their ability to communicate, as could many others. Perhaps the point is sufficiently well-made. Our Aristotelian concepts have been all wrong biblically, historically, and experientially.

What does this mean? It does not mean we should seek amazing experiences like these. We should seek God alone. Rather, it tells us we must change our attitudes and consequent treatment of animals. They are to be greeted not as mere objects, but with equanimity and respect. As we do so, and as we grow in Christ and our hearts become more like His, in our presence animals may become more like God designed them to be. They may consider us friends instead of enemies — gentler and more easily tamed, enabled to convey their needs more clearly, and to sense and respond to ours as well. They may become more intelligently cooperative with God's purposes for our life together in His good earth. Best of all, their response toward us can be a witness to the world around us, convicting hearts and minds that there is a loving God who orders His universe.

Animals may respond more readily to our leadership if we understand that our commission to "rule over" them (Genesis 1:28) does not mean they are deserving of lesser treatment. Animal intelligence and feelings are to be respected. Animals are not to be domineered and controlled like robots. They are ours to command, but the same principles Jesus laid down for those who would lead or be chief over other humans are to be applied to ruling over animals. Being masters means being humble servants. The Osage Indians of my heritage said, "They are our little brothers and sisters, whom Wahkontah (their name for God) has commanded us to take care of." Many Christian saints and theologians have said similar things — not that animals should be regarded as equal with humans, who alone are made in God's image, but that they are to be related to as fellow creatures, and not as mere objects, or "machines," as Decartes called them.

Animals' intelligence is to be respected and cultivated. That does not merely mean to be taught "circus tricks," done monkey-see, monkey-do. It means something we have not yet begun to learn — to set each creature free to express its own God-given propensity to glorify Him. The sin which we have allowed to diminish us has diminished our fellow creatures. But St. Francis of Assisi so purified his heart through a lifestyle of prayer and repentance that the birds and animals sat in rapt attention as he preached, and even the fishes gathered in swarms beneath the surface of the water to hear him!

Some might say, "This sounds oddly intriguing, but what good was it? How could this have furthered the message of the cross and salvation?" It did so by providing a witness of God's work through His creation. One of Francis' disciples, St. Anthony of Padua, was being heckled by rowdy heretics. So, like his teacher before him, he turned toward a spot where a river joined the sea, and bid the fish to listen. They quickly gathered and stood at attention, heads above water. Witnessing their obedience, many of the heretics felt ashamed of their own behavior, repented, and returned to sound doctrine![52]

Of course, few of us will display God's dominion in such a striking and unusual way. But do our relations with animals at least enable them to interact more peaceably and lovingly with us than the world has previously witnessed? Francis once said, "Let all brothers preach by their deeds."[53] When we relate with the natural world, are we preaching?

We have suppressed animal intelligence more than we have set it free.

It is time for paradigm changes in our concepts and relationships with animals.

---

[52] Ghezzi, Bert, *Mystics and Miracles* (Chicago, IL: Loyola Press, 2002), 104.
[53] McClosky, Fr. Pat, O.F.M., "Where Did St. Francis Say That?" *AmericanCATHOLIC.org*, http://www.americancatholic.org/messenger/oct2001/Wiseman.asp, 1996 (accessed Aug. 28, 2012).

CHAPTER FIVE

"HEALING" THINGS

Our Lord was asked when He would return, and what it meant that the scribes say that Elijah must come first. "And He answered and said, 'Elijah is coming and will restore all things'" (Matthew 17:11). In the Greek, "all things" (*pas*) means "all that there is." Christ came to restore not only humans, but all of creation. That includes objects.

We do not think of created things as Jesus does. Our Lord related to things that do not breathe or move, whether plants or "lifeless" objects, as though all could somehow "hear," "understand" and "obey." Listen to Scripture:

When He got into the boat, His disciples followed Him. And behold, there arose a great storm on the sea, so that

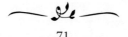

the boat was being covered with the waves; but Jesus Himself was asleep. And they came to Him and woke Him, saying, "Save us, Lord; we are perishing!" He said to them, "Why are you afraid, you men of little faith?" Then He got up and rebuked the winds and the sea, and it became perfectly calm. The men were amazed, and said, "What kind of man is this, that even the winds and the sea obey Him?" (Matthew 8:23-27).

The disciples noted that "...even the winds and the sea **obey** Him." In the Greek, the verb, "obey" (*hupakouo*), means "to listen and attend, and so to submit, to obey."[54] Some might view the wind and waves "obeying" as an anthropomorphism. But if so, why was Jesus' approach so relational? He did not speak or command **that** the winds and waves should be still. He spoke directly **to** them as one would to a human servant or work animal. Let's leave aside for the moment questions such as: how can such things "hear"? With what "ears"? With what will to obey? I cannot answer that. Our western mindset requires logical answers to all questions, but God's way is to leave some things a mystery. But one thing we can be sure of is that God gave all authority to Jesus (Matthew 28:18), and He passed that same authority on to us: "He who believes in Me, the works that I do, he will do also; and greater works than these he will do; because I go to the Father" (John 14:12b).

Many Christians have exercised this authority to heal or command nature. A friend and I were flying from Seattle to Spokane. The stewardess came on the intercom to say that

---

[54] W. E. Vine, M.A., *Vine's Expository Dictionary of New Testament Words* (Iowa Falls, IA: Riverside Book and Bible House, 1940), 806.

there were great storm clouds ahead. They could not fly over, around or under them, so it would be a very bumpy ride, and they could not serve refreshments. My friend and I conversed a moment and agreed that the Lord was prompting us to intervene in prayer. In Jesus' name, in a quiet voice I spoke to the winds and commanded them to be still — and it became perfectly calm. We landed in Spokane without experiencing even one little bump (the stewardess was quite embarrassed and puzzled). How did the winds "hear" me? I haven't the faintest idea, and I don't need to know. I just know that either they did, or that God heard on their behalf, and moved them to respond.

Years ago, Bishop Topel of Spokane, Washington, gave permission for me, a Protestant pastor, to be spiritual director for nuns in his diocese. I had taught them that in Jesus' name we have authority over winds and fire, and I shared several testimonies. Their residence had been one of the old officers' houses at Fort Wright Academy in western Spokane. A fire broke out in the valley below (their house stood at the edge of a hill). The flames were racing up the hill through dry brush, impelled by wind. One of the Sisters stood at the crest of the hill, facing the oncoming flames, and commanded them, in Jesus' name, to stop. Did anyone ever hear of flames in dry brush, driven by a strong wind, suddenly stopping!? The flames died out, and the nuns' house was saved. In Jesus, we have authority!

While I served as a pastor in Council Grove, Kansas (1961-1965), Harry White and his two nephews gave to the Kansas Conference of the United Church of Christ, 117 acres of land surrounded on three sides by water, for a church camp for young people. On the east was Monker's Creek and on the west, the Neosho River, both now swollen into a lake by the dam built below their confluence. Soon after the camp was built, a tornado arose. It was travelling from the east, heading across the water toward the middle of the campgrounds and buildings. I asked permission from God and then spoke in His name to the tornado, commanding it not to come onto White Memorial Camp. Years later when I shared about this, a man said to me, "John, that was no miracle that it missed the camp; tornado funnels don't usually travel over water." What he didn't know is that the funnel crossed halfway across the lake from the Monker's Creek side — and then stopped! Instead of crossing over the camp, it turned and went south over much water past the point of the camp, then west a bit, and turned north over a lot more water until it came to its original trajectory. At that point, although it would have been easier to have turned back east over the campground, it turned fully west, continued across the lake and onto the lands beyond, where there were no houses. That tornado "obeyed" the command not to traverse the campground and, in the process, travelled over water three times farther than it would have taken to just go straight onto the campground! We have authority, and winds and storms will obey us.

But we need to be careful that whatever authority we exercise is in obedience to what the Lord Jesus wants. I flew into Boston where a friend picked me up. We drove through Massachusetts on the way to Whitinsville where we were to conduct a School of Pastoral Care. On the way, I asked her, "How come the trees are 'crying?'" (By a word of knowledge the Lord had revealed to me that they were in distress.) She replied, "A group of us intercessors became concerned about the tropical storms and hurricanes that were coming on land here every two or three years on average, blowing trees down and doing great damage. We rose up in our authority and commanded the hurricanes not to come in [they hadn't inquired of the Lord whether it was alright to do this], and they haven't come in for eight years. We didn't know those hurricanes brought much-needed rain water. We've had a drought now for eight years! That's why the trees are suffering."

That raised a question. Did the intercessors prevent the storms by their own fleshly authority? God gave us dominion over the earth (Genesis 1:26), and by that authority, we do have the power to affect the weather through natural means (for instance, by reducing rainfall through de-forestation). But do we have the same power in the spiritual realm, even outside of God's will? Certainly not, if nature can respond only to commands made according to God's will. If we could command nature to do things outside of God's plan, it would seem that any skilled occultist could conjure storms or sunny weather, and I have never heard of this happening. I prefer to believe that God alone controls the weather, for as the Scripture states, "The earth is the Lord's, and all it contains" (1 Corinthians 10:26). Throughout the Bible we see God directing the powers of nature; nowhere do we see humans doing this, except in God's will and on His behalf.

I believe that God Himself prevented the storms in answer to the intercessors' prayers, and that this was within His permissive, though not perfect, will. If this had affected New England's water supply we would not believe this could be so, for it is not in His nature to punish millions to provide an object lesson for so few. However, the normal seasonal rains had maintained an adequate water supply for human use. Only the wilds were suffering, and even there the damage was hardly beginning. The hard lesson the Lord taught the intercessors was that if they had enquired of God before they prayed, this predicament might have been averted.

Authority must be under God's authority. Many times, I have felt grieved when farmers have commanded rains not to come, or to come to their farm but not somewhere else, without asking the Lord about what His will would be, or considering what other places or farms might have needed the rains. What might God have said? Our wisdom is not His, and we can miss opportunities to procure His blessings if we do not exercise authority under His command, within His will.

Expanding the Vision through His Call to Pray for the Restoration of All Things

Everything we make is composed of materials extracted from the earth. Therefore, since both good and evil can affect the earth, they can also affect the objects we produce (and ultimately, productivity in business). For instance, objects, even machines, can become demonically influenced. When Paula and I were writing the book, *Healing the Wounded Spirit*, we owned a timeshare in Hope, Idaho, a beautiful place where we could get away to write without constant interruptions from "devil telephone." We took two brand-new computers and their printers with us. I was writing the chapter, "Occult Involvement" (now Chapter Seven in *God's Power to Change*), which reveals how demons operate through sorcery, astrology, Satanism,

etc. I finished the chapter and pressed the command to print. The printer went crazy! It printed those marks, /#@*!*/, like cartoonists use to express curse words. I pressed the command to stop, and it went right on cursing at me — for two whole pages! I couldn't get it to quit. Finally, I unplugged it — and it still hurled a few more marks at me before coming to a stop! It didn't take a great revelation from God to know what had happened. We cast a demon out of it, and the machine worked perfectly from then on.

Can you imagine what it would be like if all business and factory owners knew to pray for the artifacts of their businesses, and enlisted the prayers of knowledgeable Christians? Not merely to ensure profits (there is nothing wrong with making a profit if one is not trying to "use" prayer for selfish ends), but for the safety of His people. How many accidents and tragedies could have been prevented if God's people had been instructed on how to hear Him and obey His calls to pray for protection concerning all things — factories, cars, trains, airplanes, etc.?

Productivity is good. Proverbs 27:18 says: "He who tends the fig tree will eat its fruit." How much productivity and how many good materials have been lost due to mechanical fractures and breakdowns? Can healing of the earth also include those things? Many times the Holy Spirit has alerted me and others that machines were about to break down, and/or harm could happen to workers. God knows all things before they happen. Like any good father, He desires to protect His children. But we have not normally thought that He wants to be invited into such mundane and "secular" things as the "healing" of machines or the prevention of mechanical disasters, if we would only hear and obey.

Many spiritual leaders have learned the wisdom of having a number of prayer intercessors who watch over them. This has proven to be of inestimable value — providing blessing, prophetic words, advice, protection, comfort, healing, etc. But what if there was intercessory prayer cover for every one of the "seven mountains," as Bill Bright and Loren Cunningham have dubbed them? (The seven mountains are designated areas of concern among Christians who take seriously God's call to workplace ministry. They are: religion, family, media, government, arts and entertainment, business and education.) What if, for example, every musical composer had a team of intercessors assigned to him by God? What heavenly music might result, and/or cacophonous and irreverent sounds prevented? How wonderful that would be!

Many inventions and discoveries have been inspired due to fervent prayer. For instance, through prayer and faithfulness, George Washington Carver helped to transform the economy of the southern U.S. After the Civil War, cotton was depleting the soil of its nutrients, and the boll weevil was devouring the cotton. George suggested alternating cotton with soybeans and peanuts to replenish the soil's nitrogen.[55] The trouble was that people could eat only so many peanuts. Farmers' initial excitement was dampened by racial hatred (Carver was the son of former African slaves) when mountains of peanuts began to rot in warehouses. Within just one week of hearing

---

[55] "George Washington Carver Biography," *bio.truestory*, http://www.biography.com/articles/George-Washington-Carver-9240299 (accessed July 6, 2012).

their complaint, George devised dozens of uses for peanuts. Eventually, he invented more than 300 products, including face cream, soap, shampoo, ink,[56] rubber, llnoleum, insecticide and gasoline.[57] By 1938, peanuts were a $200 million dollar industry.

George also invented more than 115 products from the sweet potato, including starch, flour and synthetic rubber, and from the pecan he invented over 75 products. He devised ways to make rope from discarded corn stalks, veneers from palmetto root, and synthetic marble from wood shavings. From common clays he invented dyes and paints. During World War 1, he replaced textile dyes from Europe with 500 shades of American dyes. After the war, he found a way to produce paints and stains from soybeans. Henry Ford invited him to Dearborn, Michigan, where George invented synthetic rubber out of goldenrod, a common weed. Later, Thomas Edison invited him to work at his laboratory in Orange Grove, New Jersey. George was even asked to present his findings to Congress![58]

What was George's secret? First and foremost, he lived like Jesus lived. He was known for his exceptional piety and humility. When Edison offered him an annual salary of $100,000 by some estimates (astronomical wealth in that day) and a state-of-the-art lab, he passed it up rather than abandon his disadvantaged African American students at Tuskegee Institute. He patented only three of his inventions, saying, "God gave

---

[56] "George Washington Carver," *The Great Idea Finder*, http://www.ideafinder.com/history/inventors/carver.htm, 2006 (accessed July 6, 2012).
[57] Dao, Christine, "Man of Science, Man of God: George Washington Carver," *Institute For Creation Research*, www.icr.org/article/science-man-god-george-washington-carver/ (accessed Oct. 26, 2012).
[58] "George Washington Carver," (accessed July 6, 2012).

them to me; how can I sell them to someone else?" Near the end of his life, he donated more than $60,000 of his savings to the George Washington Carver Foundation, so that others could carry on his work.[59]

Secondly, George appealed to God for scientific inspiration. George said, "God is going to reveal to us things He never revealed before if we put our hands in His. No books ever go into my laboratory. The thing I am to do and the way of doing it are revealed to me." At a meeting in New York in 1924, He said, "I never have to grope for methods. The method is revealed at the moment I am inspired to create something new... Without God to draw aside the curtain I would be helpless."[60]

For this, George patiently endured scorn from the press — two days later, the New York Times published an article called, "Men of Science Never Talk That Way." It accused him of "...a complete lack of the scientific spirit," and warned that his actions would discredit his race and the Tuskegee Institute.[61] George politely responded that he did not mean he relied on divine inspiration alone: "Inspiration is never at variance with information; in fact, the more information one has, the greater will be the inspiration." Apparently, though he took no books into the laboratory, he was well-read beforehand. But the point is that he was not bound by the popular paradigms in which

---

[59.] "George Washington Carver," *The Great Idea Finder*,
http://www.ideafinder.com/history/inventors/carver.htm, 2006 (accessed July 6, 2012).
[60.] "George Washington Carver Quotes," *blackmissouri*,
http://www. blackmissouri.com/digest/george-washington-carver-quotes.html, Feb. 3, 2008 (accessed July 6, 2012).
[61.] Liester, Mitchell B., M.D., "George Washington Carver, Scientist and Mystic," *customers.hbci.com*, http://customers.hbci.com/~wenonah/new/g-carver.htm, 1995 (accessed October 4, 2012).

the book-knowledge of his era was mired. He went on to say, "I thoroughly understand that there are scientists to whom the world is merely the result of chemical forces or material electrons. I do not belong to this class."[62]

Thirdly, George regarded nature with the same love and respect we have been speaking of. He observed that this enabled the earth to respond as God had designed:

> Many are the tears I have shed because I would break the roots or flowers of some of my pets while removing them from the ground, and strange to say all sorts of vegetation seemed to thrive under my touch until [even as a boy] I was styled the plant doctor.

Jesus said that the pure in heart shall see God (Matthew 5:8). The love George felt for the earth was an expression of that purity, and enabled him to recognize God's genius reflected in nature, as we see in the following quotes:

> Never since have I been without this consciousness of the Creator speaking to me through flowers, rocks, animals, plants, and all other aspects of His creation.

> I love to think of nature as an unlimited broadcasting system, through which God speaks to us every hour, if we will only tune in.[63]

---

[62] McMullen, Emerson Thomas, "George Washington Carver and Other Christians Who Were Scientists," *oocities.org*, http://www.oocities.org/etmcmullen/CARVER.htm, 1999 (accessed October 27, 2012).
[63] "George Washington Carver Quotes," (accessed July 6, 2012).

Healing The Earth

I am convinced that without his pure heart and love for the earth, George could never have made so many wonderful discoveries, for these virtues attune our ears to hear God when He divulges the secrets of His creation. What if all Christian inventors and scientists shared this outlook? And what if each one was covered in prayer by like-minded partners who could pave the way and open the doors for products that could bless all of mankind?

Our Lord has the keys. The Bible describes Jesus as, "He who is holy, who is true, who has the key of David, who opens and none will shut, and who shuts and no one opens" (Revelation 3:7). Our gracious, ever-polite Lord wants to open doors to inventions or to close doors on possible harm, but He awaits invitation — our hearing and obedience. He will not violate our will. We must wake up and invite Him. The Bible prophesies that knowledge will expand in the end times (Daniel 12:4). All of us have witnessed that prophecy being fulfilled, as knowledge has increased so exponentially that it's difficult for practitioners in most any field to keep up with advances. But, if God's people were assigned and diligent in prayer, imagine how much more could be accomplished — and to the glory of God.

What if every politician had a corps of intercessors dedicated to his protection and guidance? The laws politicians make either bless and protect, or lay waste and destroy the earth and its resources. Rev. Ken Wilde leads a house of prayer next to Capitol Hill. His intercessors regularly pray for all the senators and congressmen. Would that there were more, and in every state capitol! Should there not be a province of prayer for the healing of every one of the "seven mountains" and for the earth as well?

The possibilities are endless. Earlier, I quoted Matthew 17:11 where Jesus said, "Elijah **is coming** [that is, before Jesus' return — note the present tense, in Greek as well as in English] and will restore **all things**" (emphasis added). Note again, "**all** things." Do you suppose Jesus meant that Elijah by himself would do all that? Or is it God's intention to also involve many Christians in a task much like that of Elijah, as He did with John the Baptist (Matthew 11:14)? Is this not the very thing we are speaking about in this chapter? Oh, God, enlarge our vision! Call us beyond ourselves for the restoration of all things!

In Isaiah 54:2, the Lord exhorts, "Enlarge the place of your tent; stretch out the curtains of your dwellings, spare not; lengthen your cords and strengthen your pegs." We have long used that text in what is popularly called a "*rhema*" way, to encourage ourselves to venture into great undertakings. How about enlarging our vision and our calling to restore all things? How about stretching our understanding of earth and our authority in it? How about lengthening our fields of prayer and strengthening our grasp of what God may be calling us to do, not only in the marketplace, the halls of music and the machines of industry, but also in the lands on which we dwell.

Cleansing House and Land

Lands and houses are not just dead matter, unaffected by what happens in and on them. They often need to be cleansed through blessing and repentance. This is not something new and strange to us. For instance, Isaiah 33:8a-9 (NIV) says: "The treaty is broken, its witnesses are despised, no one is respected. The land mourns and wastes away, Lebanon is ashamed and withers; Sharon is like the Arabah, and Bashan and Carmel drop their leaves." Broken treaties literally dry up the land and cause trees to cast their leaves! Could this be why, in the 1930's, as the United States continued to break treaty after treaty with Native Americans, the land turned into a dustbowl? Many Christians on business or ministry trips have long known that if they want to sleep well, they must pray to cleanse their hotel rooms of deposits from the sinful activities or troubled emotions of previous occupants. Cleansing and blessing homes, churches and properties is a centuries-old practice carried on by Catholics, Orthodox, Lutherans, Anglicans and various other Protestant groups.

This practice has plenty of Scriptural precedent. Every year on the Day of Atonement, Jewish priests not only made sacrifices for the people's sins, but also sprinkled some of the blood on the horns of the altar "to cleanse it and to consecrate it from the uncleanness of the Israelites" (Lev. 16:19, NIV; see also Lev. 8:15). In Nehemiah 12:30 the priests and Levites purified not only themselves and the people, but also the gates and walls of Jerusalem. When Tobiah defiled the temple by illegally setting up residence there, Nehemiah not only expelled him but also cleansed the premises (Nehemiah 13:9). Hezekiah cleansed the temple after many generations of idolatry (2 Chronicles 29:15-18). In Ezekiel 43:20-27, for seven days the altar was cleansed from the defilement of the people's sins (see also Ezekiel 45:18-20).

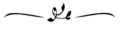

Because the new covenant no longer requires animal sacrifices for cleansing, we tend to ignore these stories. But the *original reason* for these rituals and sacrifices has not changed. It is still true that "**...bloodshed pollutes the land**, and atonement cannot be made for the land on which blood has been shed, except by the blood of the one who shed it" (Numbers 35:33, emphasis added). Hebrews 9:22 says, "The law requires that **nearly everything** be cleansed with blood, and without the shedding of blood there is no forgiveness" (emphasis added). In Old Testament times, the blood of bulls and goats symbolically substituted for our own. Today, Christ's blood is our substitute. We can ask Him to cleanse both us and the land.

A friend of mine was a real estate promoter in the state of Washington. He wanted to develop a ridge, placing houses around three sides, each with a wonderful view of the Spokane Valley. Though geologists said there ought to be plenty of water, no matter how many wells he dug, he couldn't find any. Finally, he decided that this must be something spiritual. He called and asked me to walk on the land. Sometimes the Lord gifts His people with the ability to sense the history of a piece of property — actually, just an example of the operation of the word of knowledge, one of the gifts of the Holy Spirit (I Corinthians 12:8). The Lord opened my eyes, and I "saw" that the ridge had been a favorite meeting and dancing place for a local Indian tribe. They had been cheated out of the land. A curse had been spoken over it.

Scripture clearly teaches that it is possible for one member of a group to repent on behalf of the group as a whole. For instance, in Exodus 34:9, we see Moses repenting on behalf of the nation of Israel: "Let the Lord go along in our midst, even though the people are so obstinate, and pardon our iniquity and our sin, and take us as Your own possession." Nehemiah did the same in Nehemiah 1:6 (NIV): "I confess the sins we Israelites, including myself and my father's house have committed against you." Similar prayers are found in Jeremiah 7:20 and Daniel 9:4-19. (Of course, such prayers do not eliminate the need for others to repent for their own sins, but it does stop the reaping of harm that affects a group collectively.)

Being both Native American and Caucasian, I could repent and pray forgiveness from both sides. So, as a white man, I repented for our having taken the land unfairly. I also forgave, and repented of resentment from the Native American side, and by authority I broke the curse from both sides! Within two weeks, the promoter found a good supply of water and subsequently built his houses — which became a blessing for all who lived there and enjoyed gazing at God's good earth.

A couple came to me who had never before been bothered by marital troubles, but now they were quarreling. I asked some of our usual interview questions: as children, had they been able to honor their fathers, mothers and siblings? Did they harbor bitterness toward any of them, which they were now projecting on each other? This couple had come from unusually good homes; their quarreling didn't "fit." Then the Lord prompted me to ask how long they had lived in their present house.

"Three years.'"

"How long have you been quarreling?"

"Three years."

"What is the history of what happened to the previous

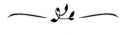

owners?"

All three couples who had previously occupied the house fought and divorced. A deposit had been left. Demons are often attracted to places where much sin has been committed. For instance, Revelation 18:2b says: [Babylon] "has become a dwelling place of demons and a prison of every unclean spirit." The passage goes on to reveal that this was a result of the many sins and adulteries committed there. In the couple's new house, demons exacerbated normal disputes into acrimonious quarrels and fights. We exorcised the house and asked the Lord Jesus to walk through its history to heal and cleanse. The couple lived "happily ever after."

Our actions either bless or defile the lands and houses (and other buildings) where we live. In turn, whatever has been deposited either blesses or defiles us. Consequently, it will not suffice just to heal people while leaving land and buildings untouched by prayer. People can become re-defiled — tempted by the spiritual influence exerted by those deposits — and so return to their sinning. Or the reverse: if we cleanse the land and buildings, but the people remain unrepentant and thus unchanged in their behaviors, they will re-defile the environment. It can form a downward spiral. Both the people and the land must be healed, together.

In our book, **Healing the Nations**, Paula and I applied this teaching to both the histories of peoples and the deposits these had left in the land. The Church needs to hear and respond to the Lord's call to heal nations as well as things. More about this later. (*Healing the Nations* can be ordered through Elijah House.)

Healing The Earth

When will we begin to realize the enormity of our calling? How long before we enlarge our vision to include the restoration of animals, objects, buildings, lands and nations? Our task will not end until the time when our Lord returns, places his people in a new earth, and fulfills the prophecies of Isaiah 11:1-9, at which time, "They will not hurt or destroy in all My holy mountain, For the **earth** will be full of the knowledge of the Lord as the waters cover the sea" (verse 9, emphasis added).

CHAPTER SIX

The Depths Of The Problem — Part One

INDIVIDUAL AND CORPORATE MENTAL STRONGHOLDS

In each previous chapter, we have said that if we do not undergo a shift in our thinking, we will lack major tools necessary for healing the earth. A primary problem is mental strongholds, individual and corporate, which affect our behavior toward the earth and its inhabitants. 2 Corinthians 10:4-5, (NIV) states:

> *The weapons we fight with are not the weapons of the world. On the contrary, they have divine power to demolish strongholds. We demolish arguments and every pretension that sets itself up against the knowledge of God, and we take captive every thought to make it obedient to Christ.*

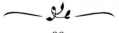

In this passage, the Greek word translated, "thought," is *noema*. A *noema* is not a mere passing thought; it is a permanent "purpose," or "device of the mind."[64] Thus, an individual stronghold is a practiced way of thinking and reacting, ingrained and automatic. We don't have to think about whatever arises within its field of operation; our response has already been built in, and is usually done unconsciously as a routine "knee jerk" reaction.

For example, my wife, Paula's, family had a practiced way of thinking and reacting which I called "the perfect squelch." Whenever someone was confronted about an offense, no matter how lovingly, or became the butt of even a well-meaning joke, the response was automatic. Within a few moments (during which one could feel that person's mental wheels turning), out would come a caustic retort designed to throw back onto the other person whatever was perceived as a put-down ("Well, you're not so hot yourself!"). Paula's family has since come to realize how hurtful this was, and have taken steps toward changing through personal healing and reconciliation. But meanwhile, this made times when Paula and I needed to talk out disagreements difficult, to say the least, and occasionally almost impossible. Together we saw that stronghold, repented of it and its origins, broke its power, and set Paula free.

The functions of a mental stronghold are to maintain control over its host, prevent him or her from seeing its grip, imprison thinking and behaviors to follow its path only, and block out truth, either from the Bible or from sound reason. It is a way that

---

64. W. E. Vine, M.A., *Vine's Expository Dictionary of New Testament Words* (Iowa Falls, IA: Riverside Book and Bible House, 1940) 1,154.

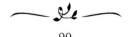

we either deliberately or unconsciously refuse change, which becomes a rut of thinking that kicks into operation faithfully each time a particular subject comes up.

On the good side, our ability to form mental ruts is God's design. If we had to think how to place our tongue and project sounds on our palette every time we wanted to speak, we could never carry on a conversation! Each time we wanted to walk, if we had to think again **how to**, we could never manage to mobilize our legs without interminable delay. It's His blessed economy that, once we have learned something and built it into ourselves, it remains, and functions whenever needed. The ability of our minds to learn skills and relegate them to automatic responses is what enables us to function in all our living.

Those habitual ways of thinking and acting are not strongholds. Strongholds are harmful fleshly constructs in our minds which result in character flaws and sins. Strongholds imprison, control, block out and manipulate. However much we may struggle to reform our thinking and reshape our behavior into righteous ways, it doesn't work when strongholds are in force. Flesh can't redeem flesh. Whenever we express or do anything of virtue, it is God's Spirit at work in us ("For it is God who works in you to will and to act according to His good purpose" — Philippians 2:13, NIV). Therefore, any degree of change for the better must be the work of the Holy Spirit. We can't take credit for it. Whatever God produces sets free. It is the opposite with strongholds. Whatever is of carnal flesh imprisons. The difference is freedom: "Where the spirit of the Lord is, there is liberty" (2 Corinthians 3:17).

Strongholds develop a life of their own, and don't want

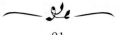

to stop operating when we want to change, even long after we are born anew. From the moment of our conversion, there is warfare within us: "I joyfully concur with the law of God in the inner man, but I see a different law in the members of my body, waging war against the law of my mind" (Romans 7:22-23a). The renewed mind of Christ within us wants to bring all our fleshly ways of thinking and acting to death on the cross. The carnal mind, built into us before we were born anew, wants to preserve its life; it does not want to die. For this reason, Paul wrote in Romans 12:2a, "And do not be conformed to this world, but **be transformed by the renewing of your mind**" (emphasis added). And in Colossians 3:9, "Do not lie to one another, since you laid aside the old self **with its evil practices**" (emphasis added). Our practiced ways of wrong thinking and acting must be reckoned as dead on the cross (Romans 6:11) if we are to be enabled to live as Christ-like Christians — or to restore the earth.

Perhaps another example may make the operation of individual mental strongholds more recognizable and understandable: in my family, a practiced way of thinking arose that was deceptive. We would get an impulse (or a temptation) to do something, and then our carnal minds would go to work developing all the reasons why we had come to that decision, excusing it to the max. The problem was that we thought we had come to that decision objectively — that this was logical and reasonable. In actual fact, the decision had already been made emotionally, even subconsciously, and our minds had become the servants of our emotions, justifying and convincing us that this was an objective and rightful choice. This was a reversal of God's order. His plan is that we are to be ruled by the Holy Spirit, prompted by Him. But our family's stronghold prompted decisions, and the renewed mind abdicated its position and deferred to the old carnal mind, justifying what our emotions had already decided — all the while convincing us we were being objective and logical.

Can you imagine how this deceptive stronghold operated between Paula and me? I would come to a false conclusion, demanding she accept it as logical and therefore right. Her keen discernment would sense something was wrong, and she would try to make me aware of that. But I would logically wear her down, unable to hear the truth behind what she was trying to say. That threatened Paula, and out would come the "perfect squelch." We're a walking miracle! God had to bring our strongholds to death so we could hold a righteous discussion — about anything.

All of us in the Western world grew up under the influence of two major corporate mental strongholds (see explanations of these in Chapter Seven) which have become individual strongholds that we did not have to build into ourselves; we absorbed them just by living in our culture.

The ways we think about and react to nature and all its animals, plants and objects, have been built into us until they are unconscious and automatic.

That is why I have so many times asserted that we are going to have to undergo dramatic paradigm shifts if we are to approach nature as our Lord Jesus did and wants us to.

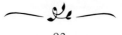

Not merely "shifts." We are going to have to see many things that our carnal minds may not want us to accept, and bring our corporate strongholds to death on the cross, appropriating, at deeper levels, resurrection into the fullness of the mind of Christ.

Corporate Stronghold:
Insensitivity to Anything Beneath Us
in the Order of God's Creation

We know ourselves to be rulers over all creation, which is biblically true. But we most often exercise that headship without respect for God's will or the worth of other creatures. For example, as I mentioned earlier, when hunting, my Osage ancestors prayed for Wahkontah (their name for God) to give to them the life of an animal. Then, having killed, they apologized to the spirit of the animal, and gave thanks. Our modern mentality sees that as mere superstition. Natives thought of animals as their little brothers and sisters, to be taken care of (does that not sound like something from the Garden of Eden?). They would not kill for sport; only for necessity. We kill for sport, make trophies of our insensitivity, and think nothing of it. That's just the way our strongholds automatically cause us to think and act.

We treat creation and all its creatures as though they are mere objects to be used, killed or exterminated at our whim, irrespective of what God may desire. Because of that stronghold, we do not stop to think, for example, about what God may intend about the tree we decide to chop down, or the animal we are about to kill. I am not saying we should not hunt, or that we should cease to fell trees. But there is a sensitivity to what God may want that we do not even consider. Listening to God does not enter our stronghold-controlled minds. Perhaps, by their asking Him for the life of an animal, native people who never heard of Jesus were more righteous and pleasing to God than we who know Him, yet act without taking thought for His purposes. How can we heal nature if our ways remain insensitive and injurious?

True dominion means responsibility, so that what we do is an expression of the will of God, not the desires and greed of mankind. Our way must become His way. We will have to undergo much repentance and daily death of self (Luke 9:23) before we can truly heal God's creation.

This doesn't mean, for example, that we should halt or cripple the forest industry. God Himself called for the logging of cedars in Lebanon to help build the temple of Solomon (I Chronicles 22:12).

What it does mean is that we should put to death ways that we now take for granted, and bring to birth new ways of relating to nature.

What if government officials who map out areas of forest to harvest, and lumbermen who successfully bid for the right to that harvest (at least those who know the Lord), could sit down together to pray for God's will? God's wisdom might propose "out of the box" strategies more beneficial than their own ideas. Whatever decisions were reached might then have a much better chance of expressing God's will — and nature would not be so callously used (and often abused).

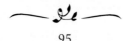

Healing The Earth

On the other hand, we can fall into unwise, slavish "obedience" in listening for guidance, whereas our Lord often wants us to combine listening with our own common sense and experiential and scientific knowledge. He doesn't want us to be robots, as though we had no other input than automatic reaction. He wants children whose free will enables them to think, ponder and make decisions in concert with Him, and thus have real fellowship with Him, even if that seems to leave doors open to possible error. A farmer tried to do absolutely everything by listening to what God would say. His own wisdom and experience said he should plant corn. But one year he thought he heard the Lord say, "Plant soy beans." It turned out to be a ruinous year for soy beans, and would have been fine conditions for growing corn. He lost hundreds of dollars and was angry at God, until I explained that the Holy Spirit wants us to use our own intelligence along with listening. What he had done was to turn listening to the Lord into divination, so as to avoid the risks of decision-making inherent in all farming. God had let him reap harm in order to teach him balance and wisdom.

As you can see, I am not advocating pat answers for relating to nature that will work every time. Rather, I am saying that changing from insensitivity to mature wisdom (in cooperation with God) is needed growth for us all. Death of our old strongholds enables the birth of new ways. New births seldom, if ever, bring forth instantly mature ways. Babies need to grow in the Lord. We are going to have to grow into the new, learning by trial and error.

Owners of factories that funnel harmful smoke into the air are going to have to be set free from strongholds of greed

and insensitivity so that conscience can live and better ways in industry can be birthed. In countries where factories still spew harmful chemicals into creeks and rivers, owners and managers are influenced by strongholds that will have to be overcome by our Lord's gentle wisdom, so they can repent and change their ways. The auto industry is in such a process regarding harmful emissions (hopefully for the right motives). But strongholds still tarry and sometimes block. There needs to be a change of heart in leadership in every field, until enough of us come to see that the old strongholds are ruinous. This is a call to Christians. Here, 2 Chronicles 7:13-14 may be truer and more applicable than in any other endeavor:

> If I shut up the heavens so that there is no rain, or if I command the locust to devour the **land**, or if I send pestilence among My people, and **My people who are called by my name** humble themselves and pray and seek My face and **turn from their wicked ways**, then I will hear from heaven, will forgive their sin and **will heal their land** (emphases added).

Most often we have quoted this scripture to call for prayers to heal the "land" as a people group or political entity. But that is not what this text is saying. The Hebrew word, *aretz*, can be used either of the physical earth or of a people group or nation; the correct meaning can only be determined by the context in which it is used. In verse 13, *aretz* clearly means "earth" ("if I command the locust to devour the **land**" — obviously, locusts would not devour a people group). Clearly then, the context indicates that in verse 14 it is the *physical* land that God is promising to heal. If enough Christians (the specific people called by His name) can catch the vision and pray, perhaps enough leaders in every field will turn from the old strongholds and enter the attempt to discover the new.

I am not naive. It is unlikely that enough Christians will read this book and the writings of others or walk in enough purity of soul to transform the entire planet. But I do hope and pray that enough of God's people, specifically His intercessors, will catch the vision and begin to pray for leaders in every field to understand what must be done, in order to affect as much healing of the earth as is possible this side of the second coming, and minimize ruinous depletion of its resources.

Corporate Stronghold:
Using the Earth's Resources Greedily and Destructively

I do not need to belabor this point; everyone is aware that many varieties of plants and animals are already extinct, or becoming so. What is important to our message here is that callous use of water, mineral deposits, plants, animals, etc., is partly due to mental strongholds, such as greed. One of the primary functions of an individual mental stronghold is to destroy the efficacy of conscience. Knowing that what we do is harmful to nature, we do it anyway — and feel no remorse, much less the kind of sorrow that leads to true repentance (2 Corinthians 7:10). For instance, men continue to tear down the rain forests of Brazil, though they know those forests are essential to the very air we breathe!

The Depths Of The Problem: Part One

Until the government stopped them, mining operations in Idaho's Silver Valley, thirty miles east of our home in Coeur d'Alene, poured hundreds of tons of spent lead ore and other debris into creeks and rivers, destroying fish and much of the wildlife in the Coeur d'Alene River and polluting Lake Coeur d'Alene. Behind this were mental strongholds that seared the conscience. The mining managers and officials were mostly good men in every other respect. Some were members of my church (when I pastored in Wallace, Idaho). Most of them would never knowingly hurt anyone. But strongholds blinded them, and kept them from acknowledging the full extent of the destruction the pollutants from the mines were causing, until the EPA forced them to build tailing ponds to purify mining waters before releasing them into creeks and rivers. To be fair, these men were managers, geologists and miners, not owners and policy makers. I know that a few were hurt and grieved, but what could they do, other than to obey — or lose their jobs? This is why I say that intercessions must rise to break the strongholds that captivate those who are ultimately in charge, and to influence government officials to act in wisdom to curtail destructive practices.

On the other hand, some in the EPA and other concerned organizations have been overcome by opposite mental strongholds of power and influence. Care for the earth can easily be perverted by a need for self-importance, diverting attention away from the real issues and onto a fight about who has the right to claim the moral high ground. But what is at stake is so much more important than ego. What if our government had not ruled that we should save spotted owls by making old-growth timber (in the northwestern U.S.) off-limits to loggers? The owls might have been driven closer to extinction, and extinction is forever. But what did saving old growth timber do? Thousands of lumber jobs were lost. In California, cutting off irrigation to certain areas of farmland was intended to save a small fish called the delta smelt from extinction (they had been inadvertently pumped to their death through irrigation pipes), but much farmland was turned into a dust bowl.

I would like to save both animals and jobs, but I will not presume to know the answers to such dilemmas. What I can say is that I see strongholds on both sides of the argument, and I suspect that these keep answers from being found. There are those who seem to care only for endangered species, with no compassion about a man's need to feed his family or the effects of their actions on the economies of entire towns. Others seem to care only for endangered jobs, sporting crass bumper stickers about spotted owl stew.

Many Christians err in this direction. I have heard some ask, "Why should we care? The delta smelt is a completely useless fish." Some have even snarled, "I don't care if the spotted owl goes extinct; people are what's important!" Sometimes our Aristotelian strongholds are as bad or worse than those of the world! Would God say, "Yes, you're right; what I created is 'completely useless'?" In the eyes of many Christians, animals have no intrinsic worth as God's creations. If they have not yet found a utilitarian use for them, they consider them "useless" objects to be discarded at their convenience.

Perhaps if God's people had repented of this mental stronghold, their prayers could have freed others from the blinding effects of their own strongholds, enabling them to find ways to save owls and protect fish without destroying production and livelihoods.

Real answers can be found only where men's and women's minds have been broken free from the captivating grip of mental strongholds, enabling them to speak the truth to one another in love (Ephesians 4:15). For that reason I write, because the Lord's intercessors must arise as an army of prayer power, so people can think rationally and freely, discuss lovingly, and find wise corporate answers to the seemingly irreconcilable problems of productivity and ecology.

Corporate Strongholds:
Aristotelian Philosophy and Docetic Theology

These strongholds have made men and women unaware of the fact that in some unexplained way all of nature has its own kind of "feelings," "hopes" and "desires." Listen carefully again to Romans 8:19: "For the **anxious longing** of the creation **waits eagerly** for the revealing of the sons of God" (emphasis added). Listen to Jeremiah 12:4: "How long is the land to **mourn** and the vegetation of the countryside to wither? For the wickedness of those who dwell in it, animals and birds have been snatched away, because men have said, 'He will not see our latter ending'" (emphasis added). Does that sound like lack of conscience? The land "longs for" and "mourns." This is a recurring theme throughout the Bible. Look up the following Scriptures; Isaiah 24:4: "The earth **mourns** and withers"; Jeremiah 4:28: "The earth shall **mourn**"; Amos 1:2: "The shepherds' pasture grounds

mourn"; and Zechariah 12:12: "The land will **mourn**" (emphasis added). That's emotion; that's sorrow and grieving, in each case because of the sins of mankind.

On the other side of it, all of creation rejoices when God redeems. Look at Psalm 96:11-13a: "Let the heavens **be glad**, and let the earth **rejoice**; let the sea roar, and all it contains; let the field **exult**, and all that is in it. Then all the trees of the forest will **sing for joy** before the Lord, for He is coming" (emphasis added).

Because of the stronghold of Aristotelianism we have thought that such expressions were mere exultant personifications of nature. But could the Bible mean it exactly as it is worded? Listen to Isaiah 35:1-2a: "The wilderness and the desert will **be glad**, and the Arabah will **rejoice** and blossom; like the crocus it will blossom profusely and **rejoice with rejoicing and shouts of joy**" (emphasis added). Do we chalk that up to mere celebrative personifying of nature? We might assume that the wilderness rejoices only metaphorically, until we recognize that it does not blossom metaphorically! Certainly the crocus will not literally "shout" (at least in a way that we can hear without the aid of the Holy Spirit — or perhaps some yet undiscovered technology). But if this is figurative, what is it figurative of? Real joy! Isaiah describes not only the flowers and the wilderness, but also the humans who have walked there as expressing the same joyful exuberance (vss. 9-10).

Earlier I mentioned what happened when the people of Almolonga, Guatemala turned wholeheartedly to the Lord. Until repentance transformed this town of 20,000, their farms hardly produced enough to subsist on. The townspeople worshipped

The Depths Of The Problem: Part One

Maximon (pronounced, "Mashimon"), the patron saint of the villages of Guatemala. Maximon was a three-foot high idol that sported a smoldering cigar or cigarette, with a hole in its mouth in which to pour liquor. People lavished it with cigars and whiskey and made pacts with it. Its priest spewed mouthfuls of booze over the people — essentially imparting the "gift" of alcoholism! Some also worshipped the idol, Pascual Bailon, the Lord of Death. Occultism and witchcraft were rampant.

The "gift" the priest spewed was not without fruit; most of the men of the town were alcoholics who beat their wives and only worked enough to buy whiskey. The town's four jails were not sufficient to hold all the inmates; some had to be bused to a neighboring city. A dismal work ethic and frequent droughts kept the number of truckloads of farm produce at a meager four a month.

While the people showered their horrid idols with kisses and affection, they chased evangelists away with sticks and rocks, and stoned the churches. Then one day, six men knocked out Pastor Mariano's front teeth and stuck a gun in his mouth. He pleaded with God to protect him; they pulled the trigger twice, but the gun wouldn't fire. From then on, he led a group of Christians in long evening prayer meetings, determined to proclaim freedom for Almolonga.

A woman asked a local pastor to pray for her violent husband, who had beaten her and then passed out. After he awoke, he gave his life to Jesus, and began converting his friends. Soon, many people were delivered from demons contracted through the worship of the idols (including a prominent priest of Maximon!). A woman who had died of gangrene was raised from the dead. She became a miracle worker, and her husband began to preach the gospel. The idols' priests gave up and went to set up shop in another town.

Eventually, the entire town was transformed. Approximately ninety percent are now Christians! Thirty-three of the town's thirty-six bars closed, and many became churches! There are now thirty churches, and several have more than a thousand members! The brothel closed, as did all four jails. Stores formerly stocked with alcohol now overflow with wholesome food. People are building sturdier houses. Streets are cleaner. Women wear fresh, new, brightly-colored clothing. Family life has dramatically improved; divorce is hardly heard of. Education has improved and literacy has increased, not only for boys, but for girls, who formerly were not allowed in school.

The town now produces 160 truckloads of produce per month instead of a mere four, transporting carrots as large as a man's forearm, basketball-sized cabbages, eight-pound beets, and radishes the size of a fist! Some vegetables that used to take sixty days to mature now take twenty-five. Droughts no longer hamper production, for underground springs have come up all around the town, keeping the soil moist. Some farmers are hiring others to work their fields, and establishing farms in other communities. Produce trucks are inscribed with phrases like, "Little Gift from God," and "Glory to God." Almolonga has been dubbed the "Valley of Miracles" and the "City of God." A sign at the entrance of the town proclaims, "Jesus is Lord of Almolonga!" Pastors have developed strategies to maintain the progress, and many Christians continue to fast and pray several times weekly to break spiritual strongholds in neighboring communities.[65]

The Lord has said that the earth would not yield its increase because of sin (Genesis 3:17 and 4:12). But in Almolonga, when repentance diminished the curse, the earth joyfully yielded. Look at Isaiah 44:23: "**Shout for joy**, O heavens, for the Lord has done it! **Shout joyfully**, you lower parts of the earth: **break forth into a shout of joy**, you mountains, O forest, and every tree in it, for the Lord has redeemed" (emphasis added). Take note of the emotions of the creation in Isaiah 49:13: "**Shout for joy**, O heavens! And **rejoice**, O earth! For the Lord has comforted His people and will have compassion on His afflicted" (emphasis added). Is it that only angels rejoice when one sinner repents? Or does God's creation join in the party? These scriptures testify that creation celebrates with God and all the angels whenever redemption occurs. There is a symbiotic relationship between mankind and nature. When mankind sins, nature mourns. When mankind is redeemed, nature rejoices.

A number of years ago, a man named Cleve Backster did experiments with plants. He headed an institute in New York that designed accurate polygraph procedures for federal police and security agencies, including the C.I.A. One day, on a whim, he attached a polygraph to a leaf on a potted rubber plant he happened to have in his office. He expected the graph to rise in an even line as the leaf absorbed water. Instead, the line wavered. He wondered if the effect would be exaggerated if one of the plant's leaves was dunked in hot coffee. He didn't actually do this, but the instant he merely *intended* to, the polygraph

---

[65] Saia, Carol, "God Ends Idol's 700-year Reign in Almolonga, Guatemala, *GlowTorch*, http://www.glowtorch.org/Home/IdolatryendsinAlmolonga/tabid/2767/Default.aspx, 2009 (accessed July 14, 2012).

jumped dramatically! Being scientifically minded, he assumed this was a mistake. To confirm this, he repeated the experiment with many different plants, using all kinds of checks and screens to avoid a false outcome, but the outcome remained the same.

In another experiment, at unpredictable intervals, he set up a computer to send impulses telling a device to dump saltwater shrimp into boiling water. Every time this happened, the plants in the next room reacted.

In order to find out if plants have memory, Cleve had a man rip apart a plant in the presence of a second plant. Later, other men walked into the room one by one, and the second plant made no reaction. Then the man who had ripped up the first plant walked in, and the second plant reacted violently!

When Winkie Pratney reported all of this in his book, *Healing the Land*, he commented, "Gardens remember cruelty. Trees record rapes. Jungles memorize murders — and murderers." And he drew a parallel with Genesis 4:10b, where God confronted Cain about murdering his brother, Abel: "The voice of your brother's blood is crying to me from the ground."

Scientists (and Backster, himself) have tried to replicate Backster's experiments, with mixed results. Backster says this may be because plants, like people, don't always react the same way. For instance, he noticed that when plants were repeatedly exposed to other plants being harmed, they stopped reacting, as if they had grown numb to it, just like people do when they are subjected to chronic abuse or trauma. Although the verdict is not yet in on just how accurate Backster's experiments are, plants do react with enough frequency to lead many to believe he was truly on to something.[66]

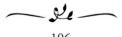

Backster also noted that plants *never* got used to harm done to humans; this always agitated them intensely. Doesn't this confirm the message of some of the Scriptures we have been quoting? The earth suffers for our welfare: "Because of this [Israel's sin], the land mourns" (Hosea 4:3a, NIV). It rejoices when we are comforted: "Rejoice, O earth! ...For the Lord has comforted His people" (Isaiah 49:13b, NIV). Should we not return the favor?

Interestingly, the experiments brought Backster closer to a Christian worldview. He remarked: "This whole thing has made me a believer in prayer. If one cell communicates like this to another, what is the effect of a whole multitude crying out?"[67]

The Bible has told us again and again that nature is affected by our emotional and spiritual state and actions, either through blessing or cursing. Again, look at Genesis 3:17-19 (NIV): "Cursed is the ground because of you. In pain you shall eat of it all the days of your life." Most people in the today's world have accepted Aristotle's view of the earth, and that has imprisoned us. Now, the Lord is setting us free.

The saints have always known that nature can hear and respond to God's voice and to commands given through His servants. Saint Francis preached to the birds, saying, "My brother and sister birds, you should praise your Creator and always love Him: He gave you feathers for clothes, wings to fly and all other things that you need. It is God who made you noble among all creatures, making your home in thin, pure air. Without sowing or reaping, you receive God's guidance and

---

[66.] Pratney, Winkie, *Healing the Land* (Grand Rapids, MI: Chosen Books, 1993), 121-127.
[67.] Pratney, 121-127.

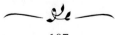

protection." The birds responded by devoting their full attention to St. Francis, spreading their wings, stretching their necks, and for all appearances rejoicing and praising God!

Francis hated to see any creature suffer, so whenever he found a fish that had been caught, he slipped it back into the water and warned it to be more careful next time. But sometimes the fish would stay awhile, listening to Francis preach, and would leave only after he dismissed them.

Around the village of Gubbio in Italy, a wolf was killing and eating people. It killed anyone who hunted it, and the villagers were terrified to leave the walls of the city. When it charged at Francis, he rebuked it: "Come to me, Brother Wolf. In the name of Christ, I order you not to hurt anyone;" and it lowered its head and laid at his feet. Then Francis said, "Brother Wolf, I want to make peace between you and the people of Gubbio. They will harm you no more and you must no longer harm them. All past crimes are to be forgiven." The wolf nodded its head and moved its body in agreement. Francis reached out his hand in pledge, and the wolf placed its paw in his hand. He then commanded it to follow him to Gubbio, where he preached repentance in the town square, then made an offering of peace on behalf of the wolf. The people promised they would feed it if it agreed not to harm them. Francis asked the wolf if it would accept this deal, and it bowed its head and moved its body in agreement, again placing its paw in Francis' hand as if in pledge. Until its death, the wolf went door to door asking for food, and harmed no one. In turn, everyone was kind to it; even the dogs would not bark at it. When it died, the people of Gubbio grieved its passing.[68]

I plead with all of us to enter into prayer and ask the

Lord to take captive all the ways we used to think in the world before we came to Him. But He will not do it all; we have a part. Our part is to recognize and repent of the ways of thinking, derived from our culture, which we have held from our youth onward. To fully do that, we need to understand what corporate mental strongholds are, and the history of how Aristotelianism and Docetism took hold of us. So keep on praying, and look for better ways as I continue to explain about corporate strongholds, in the next chapter.

---

68. Feister, John, "Stories About St. Francis and the Animals," *Seasonal Features, St. Francis and the Animals, AmericanCATHOLIC.org*, http://www.americancatholic.org/features/francis/stories.asp#bir, 1996-2012 (accessed July 7, 2012).

CHAPTER SEVEN

The Depths Of The Problem — Part Two

THE CORPORATE MENTAL STRONGHOLDS OF ARISTOTELIANISM AND DOCETISM

From earliest times a type of thinking that resembled Hindu theology prevailed among Israel's pagan neighbors and became a stronghold that controlled people's minds. That cosmology said that spirit is good and is transcendent above all, inaccessible to all but the saintliest. Matter is inherently corrupt. Mankind has fallen out of being pure spirit into the body; we have been overcome by matter — seduced and defiled. For this reason, Hindus in India believe that each person must go through various incarnations, progressively renouncing the defilement of living in a material body on a material earth, until he or she can again become pure spirit. In Bible times, belief in reincarnation was also found in some of the religions and many of the cults of the middle east,[69] and (except for the Jews) people generally believed that one had to distance himself from the material world and live a life that was purely "spiritual."

Note how opposite to Christianity this is! We did not fall out of a "pure" spiritual state to become human beings defiled by matter. We were created by a loving and wonderful God, our Lord Jesus Christ, who fashioned us with a good and holy body from the dust of the good clean earth. We do not need to renounce everything of earth. Rather, we accept Jesus Christ as our Lord and Savior, Who came in a material body to sanctify life in this material earth. We are to renounce our **sins**, not who we **are** as humans. We do not need to reincarnate; we will ascend to Heaven upon our death. The doctrine of the resurrection affirms the goodness of the earth; rather than do away with our earthly body, God will redeem it, just as He redeems our spirit. And rather than doing away with an Earth formed from "defiling" matter, God will place us in a new Earth, endowed with the same inherent goodness that Eden possessed.

Mythologies of creation throughout the Middle East expressed a sense of defilement. In the Babylonian story of creation, the god, Marduk, fights with Tiamat, his mother (note the stark contrast between their relationship and that of Jesus and His mother, Mary). Marduk stuffed the four winds down his

---

[69.] Albrecht, Mark C., *Reincarnation: a Christian Critique of a New Age Doctrine* (Downers Grove, IL: Intervarsity Press, 1982), 30.

mother's throat, whereupon she died of gas poisoning and fell to the ground. He slit her belly and her intestines fell out. He lifted up the top half; that became the heavens. The blood and guts running out at the bottom became earth — that was our creation! With that story, are we going to respect our bodies and the earth?!

Witness the Egyptian story of creation. In an ooey-gooey mud flood, hillocks arose. On one hillock, a man stood up. One version says he spat; another, that he masturbated. That spit or semen was the earth and us! Yuck!

Contrast that with what God has revealed in His Holy Word; our good and Holy Father, through His beloved Son, said, "'Let there be light,' and there was light. God saw that the light was **good**" (Genesis 1:2-3, NIV, emphasis added). For six days God created, and after each day, God saw that what He created was "good." On the sixth day, God created man and woman. Using the good clean dust of the earth, He breathed His own holy breath into Adam, and saw that all He had created was "**very good**" (vss. 4-31). What a wonderful story of creation our Lord has given us in His Holy Word! Unfortunately, that was not what occupied the minds and hearts of the nations surrounding Israel where Christianity first took hold among the gentiles. To make matters worse, in the early 300's B.C., Alexander the Great, a student of Aristotle, had conquered the Middle East and had infected local cultures (as well as the entire Greek-speaking world) with his teacher's ideas that further denigrated the material in favor of the spiritual.

But let's back up a bit, to see the problem of contrasting theologies within the context of all of history.

In the Garden of Eden, Adam and Eve, who had been created in God's image, could easily walk and talk with Him. Their hearts and spirits were perfectly attuned to His, so that whenever He came walking in the Garden in the cool of the day, they could run to Him with perfect delight, trusting His Fatherly goodness, reading His heart and receiving His love, understanding whatever He said without confusion or misunderstanding. But then Satan tempted them to drink from his own corrupt character by eating from the tree of the knowledge of good and evil.

I agree with the many scholars who suspect that if Adam and Eve had continued to walk in righteousness, eventually they would have become mature enough so that, in His own right time, God would have said, "Okay, now you can eat from the tree of the knowledge of good and evil." It's as simple as the fact that knowledge of how to drive a car is good, but, as parents, we want to wait until our children are mature enough to receive such knowledge. Had Adam and Eve not sinned, they might have eventually come to know good and evil from God's perspective. Instead, they came to know good and evil through the ways of Satan, corrupt and harmful.

Consequently, they became filled with Satan's distrust, so that when God came walking in the Garden in the cool of the day, instead of running to Him as they had before, they fled from Him Who is the very embodiment of forgiveness, and hid among the trees of the Garden (Genesis 3:1-8). What followed was buck-passing and lying, as God asked questions they could easily have answered truthfully before (a fuller exposition can be found in Chapters Six and Seven of *Life Transformed*, which I co-wrote with my son, Loren). They had become filled with Satan's ways, devious and untruthful, and God had to put them out of the Garden.

Mankind then spread over the earth, but became more and more confused and unable to perceive and receive God for Who He is. He came to His children in China, but they received only His wisdom, and knew nothing of His loving Fatherly nature through His Son, our Lord Jesus Christ. He came to His children in India, and they managed to perceive that He is a kind of trinity — but the third member was not our gentle Holy Spirit; it was Shiva, the destroyer! God approached men in Central America — and they fore-typed the blood sacrifice of our Lord Jesus, but did it by sacrificing thousands of young men!

Mankind had become mentally ill. No one could perceive the reality of God as He is. "We know that when He appears, we will be like Him, because we will see Him just as He is" (1 John 3:2, NIV). For now, we don't.

Some may object to the term, "His children," when I refer to those not yet born anew. Let me explain. All people everywhere were created as children of God. But like the prodigal whose father said in Luke 15:24, "This son of mine was dead," we died to what it means to live as sons. It is from that fall from father-child relationship that we Christians have been redeemed and born anew. Being saved gave us power to become **again** the children of God (John 1:12). He loves us as the best Father Who ever was.

If we are to comprehend God's grief, it is important to understand this. What father and mother have not experienced times when one or more of their children became confused or rebellious and could no longer understand and trust their loving approaches? It hurts when our children misunderstand and project onto us hurtful ways we have not at all intended. But in most families that happens infrequently, temporarily, and with only one or two children at a time. Imagine the hurt in the heart of our loving Father God when all of His children everywhere, all of the time, became lost from Him, and could not understand, trust and receive Him for Who He really is. If mankind were to be redeemed to see Him as He really is, God would have to send His own Son to die for us, and the Holy Spirit to teach and illumine, until all of us who would invite Him into our hearts would no longer project all manner of untruths upon Him.

Satan did not win a victory. He did not slip one up on God and force Him from plan A to plan B. God knew from the beginning, before Adam and Eve were created (and before we were born), that we would fall. From the ground plan of creation He planned to restore His people so they could again know Him and relate to Him in loving embrace. Ephesians 4:4-5 says, "He chose us in Him before the foundation of the world, that we would be holy and blameless before Him. In love He predestined us to adoption as sons through Jesus Christ to Himself, according to the kind intention of His will."

But in the meantime He came to Abraham, gave him the land of Canaan, and told him his people would have to go through 400 years of captivity in Egypt (Genesis 15:1-13). Then He came to Moses and said, "**I AM WHO I AM**" (Exodus 3:14). Thus, He began to reveal Who He really is — not the sun god, nor the moon god, nor the dog god of Egypt, but the very God of all creation Who reveals Himself to whomever He wills.

The Depths Of The Problem: Part Two

Through many plagues, signs and wonders, He brought the Jewish people out of Egypt to the foot of Mount Sinai. There, He entered into a covenant with them. If they would be His people, He would be their God. If they would be a light to the world around them, He would give them a land of milk and honey. He wanted them to be a living testimony, a demonstration of His nature to the entire Middle East and beyond. Thus He would have a people who would reveal Who He is. He could say, "Look at these people. You will see Who I am and what I am like."

To do that, He had to write His character upon their hearts. So He gave them the Ten Commandments and all the laws laid down in Exodus, Leviticus, Deuteronomy and Numbers. In Deuteronomy 6:1-15, He told them to keep all His commandments, lest "…the anger of the Lord your God will be kindled against you, and He will wipe you off the face of the earth" (vs. 15).

But it was not enough merely to know the rules. The people needed a personal relationship with their God. By way of analogy, when I was a boy, it was not enough that my mother and father gave me a list of rules to live by — hoe the garden in straight lines; don't be late to school; chew with your mouth closed. I needed more than their instructions. I needed them to talk with me, heart to heart, about the issues of life — what I felt, what I needed, how to live and how to love. Just so, the Hebrew people had to be able to hear God. He wanted to talk with all of them, even as He had visited with Adam and Eve in the Garden, but that would have to wait until their Messiah came to show them the Father. Meanwhile, they saw Moses go up on the mountain looking fairly normal, and, after many days of fire and thunder, come back down white-haired and glowing like a lamp! They were afraid, so they said to him, "Speak to us yourself and we will listen; but let not God speak to us, or we will die" (Exodus 20:19, NIV).

We all know the rest of the story. Again and again Israel failed to be the light God had wanted them to be. Because of their unfaithfulness and their fear of the giants in the land, they had to suffer forty more years in the wilderness, until an entire fearful generation of unbelievers died off, out of which only faithful and courageous Caleb and Joshua remained (Numbers 13:26-14:35). Joshua led the next generation into crossing the Jordan miraculously, and — miracle by miracle — Israel conquered until they did indeed possess the Promised Land. But they subsequently fell away from God again and again, to follow after false gods. In short, they failed to be the light and were eventually exiled from the land.

Again, Satan did not surprise God and win a victory. God knew the Israelites would fail. But He also knew they would lay the groundwork for the coming of His own Son, our Lord Jesus Christ, Who would once and for all reveal Who God is and His wonderfully loving character: "Have I been so long with you, and yet you have not come to know Me, Philip? He who has seen Me has seen the Father" (John 14:9). Through His Son, Father God would at last reveal Who He is and restore His children to loving fellowship with Him.

Through the Church, the living Body of our Lord Jesus Christ, God still carries out this plan — to show the world Who He really is. His plan extends even beyond the earthly realm,

"...so that the manifold wisdom of God might now be made known through the church **to the rulers and the authorities in the heavenly places**" (Ephesians 3:10, emphasis added). God not only wants to say to all the peoples of the world, "Look at My church, and You will see Who and What I am;" He also wants us to be a demonstration of His nature to all the angels and demonic principalities in all the heavens!

The problem was that this message was scandalous to people of the first century who could not conceive of a material Christ working through a material church. For this reason I have sketched this brief history of all mankind and God's interaction with us.

Christianity was birthed in a land suffused with strongholds of error, especially Gnosticism and Docetism.

It was considered scandalous to think that the holy God Himself would be born into a real human body. Horrors! To have to be suckled at the breast and have His diapers changed? That could not be! So Cerinthus came up with a heresy called "adoptionism." God could not have let Himself be defiled by becoming human through a woman's body, so He found a grown man and adopted him, inserting Christ's spirit into his body.

Another heresy arose that Jesus just "appeared" (in Greek, *dokein* — hence, the term, "docetism") to have a body, floated around a while, and went back up to heaven to be a pure spirit again. Can we see in this a similarity with the Hindu concept of "purity" (escape from defilement on earth) through Nirvana?

That stronghold of Docetism gripped men's minds, and

made it a horrendous struggle to believe that Jesus is truly God's Son come in the flesh. For this reason the apostle John, who saw the problem more clearly than most, said,

> *Beloved, do not believe every spirit, but test the spirits to see whether they are from God, because many false prophets have gone out into the world. By this you know the spirit of God: every spirit that confesses that Jesus Christ has come in the flesh is from God, and every spirit that does not confess Jesus is not from God; this is the spirit of antichrist, of which you have heard that he is coming, and now is already in the world (*1 John 4:1-3, emphasis added*).*

Perhaps a review of how Docetism along with Aristotelianism have waged war for men's minds throughout Christian history, will help reveal what continues to engender warfare today for the healing of all the earth.

The Apostle John battled still another philosophy that taught that God would not stoop to touch anything material lest it defile Him, for it was by its very nature corrupt. In that philosophy, the "Logos" was a lesser extension of God — an inferior intermediary between Him and the material universe. This Logos created the earth so that God could remain separate from it and undefiled. The supreme God created spiritual things; the Logos created the earth from formless pre-existing fallen material, as an imperfect and polluted copy of the perfect spiritual world.[70]

[70.] "Emanation," *New Testament Made Easy*,
http://www.newtestamentmadeeasy.com/emanation.html, 2011 (accessed July 6, 2012).

To counter this theology, the first words of John's gospel thunder: "In the beginning was the Word [John used the Greek term, *Logos*] and the Word was with God, and the Word was God" (John 1:1). (The *Logos* and God were together from the beginning; Jesus was not lesser than God — a later emanation of Him. This explodes with truth against docetic theology!) Verse 2 says, "He was in the beginning with God" (John says it again, for emphasis). Verse 3: "All things came into being through Him, and apart from Him nothing came into being that has come into being." (It was not that a supreme being created spiritual things while the Logos created lower, material things. **All** things were created by the Logos, Who became material flesh in our Lord Jesus Christ.) Verse 4: "In Him was life, and the life was the light of men." (There was no darkness of death in Him; becoming human did not make Him corrupt. He was and is full of life and purity. He is not a lesser light that confuses men; rather, He is their very life.) Verse 5: "The Light shines in the darkness, and the darkness did not comprehend it." (The light of God shines through His **material** Son with such undefiled purity that the darkness has, indeed, not comprehended, or as some versions say, "overcome" it. Instead, this light has overcome darkness.)[71] Since the docetic Gnostics had said that the lesser god had become overcome and defiled, John returned to the theme in John 1:14: "And the Word became flesh, and dwelt among us, and we saw His glory, glory as of the only begotten from the

---

71. **Note:** since the Greek word, *katelabeo*, can have more than one meaning, some versions read, "The darkness has not 'overcome' it." But there is no real disagreement between these alternate translations of *katelabeo*, for it is true that the darkness of Docetism does not "comprehend" the fact that the light of God shines through His material Son with such undefiled purity that the darkness has, indeed, not "overcome" it.

Father [not created, but begotten], **full of grace and truth**" (not mixed up and defiled, but "full of grace and truth!"). What a powerful apologetic these few verses are! They destroy docetic Gnosticism for all who have eyes to see.

But the stronghold of Docetism was not that easily expunged from early Christian thinking and beliefs. The Greek mentality had accepted the belief that, at death, we return to being pure spirits, free from the defiling body. Therefore, Paul wrote 1 Corinthians 15 to insist that we are indeed raised in a real physical body. "But someone will say, 'How are the dead raised? And with what kind of body do they come?' You fool!" (vss. 35-36a). Paul went on to discuss various kinds of bodies and their glory, and then said,

> So also is the resurrection of the dead. It is sown a perishable **body**, it is raised an imperishable **body**; it is sown in dishonor, it is raised in glory; it is sown in weakness, it is raised in power; **it is sown a natural body, it is raised a spiritual body.** If there is a natural body, there is also a spiritual body (vss. 42-44, emphases added).

Paul was saying to the Greek mentality, as clearly as he could, that we will be raised as a real physical body; it will be glorified into all that God has intended it shall be, but it will still be a very real physical body.

The Church continued to battle docetic thinking throughout the first few centuries and beyond. The battle took a different turn at the Council of Nicea in 325 A.D. There, the Aryans presented a heresy that was the opposite of Docetism, yet sprang from the

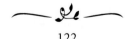

same delusions. Unlike the Docetists who believed that Jesus was God but only appeared to be human, the Aryans believed that Jesus was, in fact, human, but a created being, not co-eternal or of the same nature and essence with the Father. But the same delusion still held sway — that becoming fully human would have defiled and lowered God. Athanasius, the great ascetic hermit-turned-deacon from Alexandria, fought for true orthodox doctrine. The battle waged over one little Greek letter. Would the Nicean Creed say that Jesus was *homo-ousios* (of the same nature as God the Father) or *homo-i-ousios* (of like, but not the same, nature)? Arius argued that Jesus must be a lesser being, of like nature but not the same nature as God the Father. By God's providence, Athanasius won.Therefore the Nicean Creed reads, "God from God... one essence [nature] with the Father."

Though again and again such theologies have been defeated, they spring up anew in every century, more often as an undercurrent of thought than an expressed theology. In the 19th century, the Church was dominated by docetic thinking. In some denominations, husbands and wives were taught that sex was nasty. If you had relations, it should be only to have children. If you enjoyed it, you had sinned (and if your denomination practiced the confessional, you needed to confess to the priest).

Docetic thinking compartmentalizes life, so that if you are working at a lathe, you think that's only physical; but if you are praying, that's spiritual. One acts "spiritual" on Sunday during worship. What one does the rest of the week is only physical — working, eating, sleeping, making love, etc. **Nothing could be further from the truth!** We are spiritual beings wherever we are, whatever we are doing. **We are fully human and fully spiritual in every activity!** Sex is not nasty; it is holy when done lovingly and within marriage.

But when the stronghold of Docetism controls a man, he thinks, "I'll just go enjoy that prostitute. That has nothing to do with my spirit; it's only a body-to-body thing." Wrong! Paul said so clearly, "Or do you not know that the one who joins himself to a prostitute is one body with her? For He says, the two shall become one flesh" (1 Corinthians 6:16). A docetic-minded person might take the phrase, "one flesh," to mean that sex is just between two bodies. However, "one flesh" means so much more than that. Verse 19a asks, "Do you not know that your **body** is a temple of the Holy Spirit who is in you" (emphasis added)? In Romans 1:9b, Paul says, "I serve in my **spirit** in the preaching of the gospel" (emphasis added). If our body is the temple of the Holy Spirit, and that temple is where our spirit serves, how can it then be said that one serves God with his spirit but has sex with his body? Since our spirit dwells in our body, what we do with our body is what we do with our spirit! This is the true meaning of "one flesh."

If we thought as Jesus thinks, we could not tolerate pornography. But too often we think, "That's just a body. Why not enjoy it?" If we thought like Him, we would realize that every Christian is a temple of God's Holy Spirit and radiates His life. We could not stand to defile that glory. People say, "What's wrong with looking at its parts?" But remember, "Everyone who looks at a woman with lust for her has already committed adultery with her in his heart" (Matthew 5:28).

If people thought biblically, abortion would be recognized

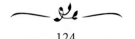

for what it is — murder — because we would know there cannot be a baby's body in a womb without its spirit in every cell. A baby does not become a living soul when it first breathes air. A baby is a living spirit within its body from the moment of conception — a living soul, not an "it." But all too many people, even Christians, don't think in these terms because the stronghold of Docetism rules their thinking and has thus blocked their conscience.

Three psychiatrists came to me, asking, "What can we do to get the Holy Spirit into our practice?" My jaw nearly fell open in shock. They did not know that their sitting and listening was itself spiritual, that God's Spirit (in theirs) ministered His love through all their counseling and prescribing. To be sure, if they had recognized and opened more fully to Him, God could have ministered through the supernatural gifts of the Spirit as well. But this is not the only way the Holy Spirit works through us. They did not have to "get the Spirit into their ministry," as though He were something apart from what they already did through who they were in everyday life. Docetic thinking had falsely compartmentalized life for them.

How does this affect the way we relate to animals, plants and objects? Ephesians 4:6 says that God the Father is "… over all and in all and through all." One might argue that "all" in this context means all Christians, but verse ten goes onto say that He fills "…all things" (the NIV translates it, "the whole universe"). "All" means **all**. Although God *is* not creation, as the Pantheists believe, God's Spirit flows *through* all of His creation, which includes all His plants and animals, and even objects. The docetic heresy held that all of nature is defiled, and even if it were not, it has nothing of God's Spirit in it because the Holy

Spirit is far above, not filling everything here on earth. Even though we reject Docetism as a theology, we may still practice it in our hearts without realizing it. If we thought in Hebraic-Christian ways, as Jesus does, we would stop callously using things, and meet nature with awe and respect. Instead, we use, abuse, maim, kill and disrespect nature and its creatures, to the point of extinction in all too many cases. There must come a total turnabout in the way we think about God's creation and all His creatures.

If we are to make that turn, we must jettison another way of thinking that has helped form the foundations of modern thought — Aristotelianism. As I mentioned earlier, in 333 B.C., Alexander the Great, a disciple of Aristotle, conquered the entire Middle East. Hellenism (Greek cultural influence) became the "in thing" (fashions, clothing, language — the New Testament was written in Koine Greek). Greek philosophies became the rage for the intelligentsia of the time, and filtered down into the common man's everyday thinking.

Centuries later, during the 1200's, Thomas Aquinas re-popularized Aristotle, and made Aristotelian logic the foundation for modern scholasticism. Once again, Aristotle's philosophy became a stronghold of thought that ruled most men's minds from then on, and still does today. It ruled in the seminary I attended, and was accepted as Christian thinking, though it so often runs counter to the Bible. As I have said, Aristotle taught that anything that does not move or breathe has no life or spirit in it. But that's a lie; creation is redolent with the Spirit of God, flowing in and through all its aspects.

Because modern (so-called "scientific") men believe

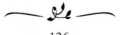

Aristotle rather than the Bible, they have no mental boxes into which they can put the idea that "...the trees of the forest will sing for joy" (Psalm 96:12), or that "...the whole creation groans and suffers the pains of childbirth" (Romans 8:22).

Perhaps, for many, conundrums such as these don't matter. The common man just believes. Questions about the scientific possibility (or impossibility) of Bible stories don't seriously hinder his faith. He just humbly thinks, "I don't understand now, but later our Lord will make things clear." Many Christians are willing to live with the jagged edges of unanswered questions and seemingly contradictory logic.

But the intelligentsia, who have been taught not to believe anything until it has been scientifically proven, think they must either take leave of what their secular studies have taught them and enter into the seeming irrationality of blind belief in the Bible, or cling to their philosophies and merely give lip service to faith, if not reject it altogether. For such people, the Aristotelian stronghold destroys any middle ground. Today, many scientifically educated people go to church because they see some good fruit from it, while their actual belief is hung in a closet of intellectual reservations until someone can make sense of the conflict between Aristotelian concepts of reality and what the Bible says.

I was invited to teach in an Episcopal Church. Its sanctuary proved to be too small for the crowds who enrolled, so the planners rented a larger church's sanctuary nearby. Neither they nor I were aware of the theology of that church. I spoke about the earth and docetic theology, as we have written here. Two young pastors of that church arose to object to all I had said. They protested, "We do not believe this way. God created this earth but is apart from it, watching it wind down like a clock. When Ephesians 4:6 says that He is "…over all and through all and in all," that does not refer to the earth but only to His being above, in and through all of us Christians. God is not in His creation, which has become defiled by mankind's sinning." (They were apparently unaware of verse ten, which, as I have said, goes on to say that Christ fills "**all things**"). I'm pretty sure these young men had no awareness of Docetism, but they had swallowed docetic thinking hook, line and sinker. I'm sure they also did not know that they had actually subscribed to a philosophy called Deism, which teaches that God only originated the universe, but is not involved in it. (It was, in fact, the deists who first invented the clock metaphor!) This is nothing like the God we know, who will not let a sparrow fall to the ground apart from His will (Matthew 10:29). But they thought that what they believed was Christian.

When Aristotelian philosophy is coupled with docetic thinking (as in the minds of these two pastors), they become two very powerful strongholds in one. Docetism compartmentalizes life into the spiritual and non-spiritual, whereas Aristotelianism conveniently "confirms" that anything that does not move or breathe has no life in it, and thus is not spiritual. The two go together hand-in-glove.

My hope is that the stories and testimonies in previous chapters have begun to open our minds. Let me be clear — that we are not yet clear! No one fully knows how we shall think about and relate to plants, animals and objects in the way Jesus intends. I am not laying out a systematic theology of earth and our relationship to it. That remains for us all to discover corporately as we explore Scripture and the wisdom of saints of the past who related to nature more scripturally than we do. But I am saying that we are tardy.

While we do not fully know what degree of healing of the earth is possible in our own lifetime, Scripture does provide a glimpse of what a new, fully healed earth will look like after His second coming. Isaiah 11:6-9 says:

And the wolf will dwell with the lamb,
And the leopard will lie down with the young goat,
And the calf and the young lion and the fatling together;
And a little boy will lead them.
Also the cow and the bear will graze,
Their young will lie down together,
And the lion will eat straw like the ox.
The nursing child will play by the hole of the cobra,
And the weaned child will put his hand on the viper's den.
They will not hurt or destroy in all My holy mountain,
For the earth will be full of the knowledge of the Lord
As the waters cover the sea.

Whew! What an impossibility! What about the precarious balance of nature, as one species feeds on another? If carnivorous foxes, wolves and snakes ceased to kill and eat, would we not soon be overrun by rodents? What if lions ceased to reduce the ranks of herbivores in Africa? And how could lions exist on a diet of grasses?

Was God speaking only figuratively through Isaiah? This

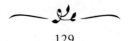

might clear up some people's confusion, but then that could not be reconciled with, "They will not hurt or destroy in all My holy mountain." Skeptics are faced with an impossible conundrum. If God's Holy Word is true, and Isaiah 11 will someday happen, the entire balance of nature will be upset, and other solutions to animal overpopulation will have to be found!

Here is a possible explanation: just as God commanded meat-eating animals not to harm other animals while both entered the ark, can He not also command future animals to change their ways? Can He not change digestive systems so a lion can indeed eat straw like an ox?

Does such thinking sound improbable, or impossible? Scientific men will have to throw away much of their learning and accept what previously seemed irrational. For those bound by the shackles of Aristotelianism and Docetism, the seemingly unanswerable questions of faith and reality will boggle the mind.

It is interesting to note that when Isaiah prophesied that in the new Earth animals will no longer kill and eat each other (Isaiah 11:6-9) he was not speaking of a first-time occurrence. This was the actual way of life in the beginning, before the Fall! We tend to take note that this was so for Adam and Eve ("Behold, I have given you every plant yielding seed that is on the surface of all the earth, and every tree which has fruit yielding seed; it shall be food for you" — Genesis 1:29), and that after the flood God gave us permission to eat animals ("Every moving thing that is alive shall be food for you; I give all to you, as I gave the green plant" — Genesis 9:3). But how many of us have noticed what Genesis 1:30 actually says? "And **to every beast** of the earth and to every bird of the sky and to every thing that moves on the earth which has life, **I have given every green plant for food**; and it was so" (emphasis added). The original command to eat only plants was given not only to humans but also to animals, and, impractical as that may seem, "…it was so"! The future condition of life prophesied in Isaiah 11 is not something new and untried; it was the successful way of all of life for both humans and animals before the fall!

That is the dramatic world of change which our Lord will re-create! He has said, "For behold, I create new heavens and a new earth" (Isaiah 65:17), in which "...the cow and the bear will graze. Their young will lie down together, and the lion will eat straw like an ox" (Isaiah 11:7).

Although this will not all occur until after the second coming, I believe that until then we are called to be part of Christ's renewing. He could have changed all our character traits from Heaven with one simple command. Instead, He became one with us, and calls us all into the process of helping each other to be transformed, as Ephesians 4:16 (NIV) says: "The whole body…grows and builds itself up in love, as each part does its work." Will He not also invite us into whatever degree of transformation of the earth is possible this side of the second coming? Romans 8:21 tells us that when the sons of God are "revealed," the creation itself also will be set free from its slavery to corruption. That "revealing" (that is, our complete transformation), will happen at the time of our resurrection (verse 23). But are we not, even now, being transformed to some degree? 2 Corinthians 3:18 says that we are presently "…being transformed into the same image [that is, God's image] from glory to glory" (emphasis added).

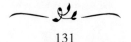

131

Healing The Earth

If our complete transformation will result in completely freeing nature from corruption, then shouldn't whatever lesser degree of personal transformation we undergo in this lifetime result in an equal degree of transformation of nature around us?

I write this book, and particularly this chapter, to call us into whatever the Lord will have us do at this time to transform the earth. For many years I have put off writing, wrestling with the questions posed in this chapter particularly — until, at last, I have come to see that we don't have to have all the answers. No one has them. We only have to have Jesus, Who holds all the answers. We only need to be obedient, to be found doing whatever He has commanded when He returns. Our task is only to open the door. The call is to all who would respond to the Lord's summons to begin the race for others to finish.

CHAPTER EIGHT

The Depths Of The Problem — Part Three

THE ENEMY – US!

Years ago there was a comic strip (still appearing in a few newspapers today) whose main character was a very human-like opossum named "Pogo." In one episode, Pogo is seen paddling his canoe out of the murky depths of the swamps, proclaiming, "We have met the enemy, and he is us!"

How true that is! Nearly forty years ago, the Lord introduced me and several others to the idea of setting nature free from its bondage to decay, and relating in Christ's love to plants, animals and objects. But then He revealed that if He were to trust us to do the work of Romans 8:21-23, setting the creation completely free before His second coming, it would be too soon — and more harmful than to let nature remain as it is. Why? Because, overall, mankind remains callous in its ways: "We have met the enemy, and he is us."

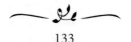

Healing The Earth

Let me share a few stories to help us understand:

I came home one afternoon and found our collie dog, Julie, waiting for me. As I stepped out of the car, she looked at me intently. Our eyes locked, and though Julie did not audibly speak the actual words, it was if she said, "I'm sick. Take me to the doctor." It was so clear that I wondered if I was hearing it with my physical ears! In case anything like this ever happens to you, I caution you to weigh your experience carefully against Scripture, and to check it out through the discernment of mature Christians, for some who do not do this may be deluded. If what I "heard" was audible, there is clear precedent in the story of Balaam's donkey. But if it was not, what was it? Telepathy? Sending or receiving a message without the voice is a tool of the occult, and forbidden by Scripture. Or was it a word of knowledge (God, not Julie, phrasing Julie's needs in words I could understand)? There may be precedent for this in Acts 16:9, where, in a vision, Paul saw a man from Macedonia saying to him, "Come over to Macedonia and help us." This was no telepathic message. Through a vision God simply portrayed in words the cry of the hearts of the people of Macedonia.

But at the moment, there was no time to ponder these questions. If what I heard was not from God, it would not hurt to take her to the vet anyway. But if it was from God, and I did not go, Julie could suffer. Immediately, I opened the car door and invited her in. I drove her to the veterinary clinic and returned home. A couple of hours later, the veterinarian called us to say, "Her entire womb was filled with pus. We've had to perform a hysterectomy. If you had brought her an hour later, it would have been too late; she would have died." God had allowed me to know what Julie needed.

I had taken a youth group to camp in a wooded area. We stretched a canvas over the place where we would sleep and eat, to protect us in case of rain. When the task of making and driving stakes was completed, I thoughtlessly stuck my hatchet into the great tree which shaded us. Instantly, I felt as if the tree had somehow "taken offense." I apologized, saying I had been thoughtless, and removed the hatchet. It was not as though I were trying to contact nature. By hindsight, the fruit tells me that God might have used this incident to speak to me (from then on I was motivated to treat nature with more care). Whether or not He did, if I had taken this experience as license to initiate two-way telepathic contact with nature, what trouble I would have reaped! Ezekiel 13:3a (NIV) says, "Woe to the foolish prophets who follow their own spirit." There are many Christians who are spiritually sensitive to nature. Such sensitivity must be tempered by knowledge of Scripture, keen discernment, and accountability to pastors and mature Christians, lest some become "pet psychics" and head into delusion!

That is not to say we should close our hearts and spirits to the refreshment nature brings. After that, as though those experiences awakened me, whenever I walked in the woods I could feel God's love coming through the trees. I learned to pronounce blessings on nature in gratitude for what God had made. I felt as if greeted by the grass and flowers as they expressed God's peace and glory. Other Christians have testified to me of similar experiences.

But be careful to avoid New Age delusions. It is good to be blessed by nature, and at times God may initiate supernatural

experiences. But do not initiate them yourself. Just follow Jesus, and make Him your focus. Evaluate anything you experience through scriptural principles. I admit that as an immature young Christian I was occasionally deluded for a short time. I know how anxious and "sweaty" those times were. The peace of God was absent, and it returned only when I repented and broke free. But I have never experienced anything other than blessing in those particular encounters with nature.

A rancher and his ranch hands were struggling to hold down a strong young bull so they could slip a powerful rubber band over his testicles. They knew the constriction would eventually castrate him. But he was thrashing so violently that all were being kicked and tossed about. I stepped in to help hold him down, and the Lord brought the following words to me, spoken as if from the bull's perspective: "I didn't think you would do that to me." Quietly, I apologized and said, "I'm sorry. I knew they would succeed in doing it anyway, so I thought if I helped, it might not be so hurtful to you." Was that only imagination? I did not invite that; I was shocked when it happened, and immediately sought the Lord about what my response should be.

I wonder how often God would like to let us know what animals are needing and feeling, if only we had ears to hear Him. I long for the day when the Lord shall have so healed us that this can happen. Many friends have told me how they are sure that the Lord has relayed to them what their animals needed to say — often a quick word of warning of some danger the animal could see but they couldn't.

I am not recommending that everyone try to have such

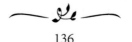

experiences. It's significant that I have *never* initiated such encounters. They happened **to** me. I share them here to reflect, that, as Hamlet said, "There are more things in Heaven and earth, Horatio, than are dreamt of in your philosophy." As I have said repeatedly, entering into the field of healing the earth will require major paradigm shifts in our thinking. We are going to have to venture beyond the comfort zones of what our philosophies have told us reality is — or what it's limited to.

Many Christians have learned to sense when the Holy Spirit is alerting them that an aspect of nature is suffering. I can feel the hurt empathetically (remember what I taught earlier about how all of nature has emotions and desire, and quoted from Romans 8:18-22). The Holy Spirit almost always prompts our daughter Ami and me to feel the same hurts in nature at the same time, and to recognize them as summons from the Lord to pray in intercession.

As I said before, the Lord has begun to teach me about healing nature. I suspect that doing so is not much different than what I shared in the testimonies I gave about healing the memories of dogs and horses. I just believe that whether or not whatever aspect of nature I am praying about can hear and understand, God hears and answers.

I think we will increasingly need humility of mind as the Lord leads us into healing the earth. "Humility of mind" may be described as flexibility, and courage to try new things, trusting in the Lord's grace to help us correct course if we err.

At one point, I foolishly taught others how to "awaken nature from sleep" (that is, restore it to all of its pre-fall capacities). In ministry to humans, I had learned that we can "fall asleep" spiritually, and how to awaken an individual's "slumbering" spirit — that is, a spirit that we have chosen to close off from love and life, and is therefore incapable of such things as hearing God, enabling us to relate heart to heart with another human being or accessing creativity. "Awakening" a tree, plant or animal to become what God intended it to be (at least as far as possible in this age) is not much different — only easier — because they are not rebellious, nor so complex and resistant, as humans.

I report this to reaffirm what I said earlier: that the Lord eventually said to me, "It's not time, John. Turn it all off." He explained that if He allowed us to awaken nature so that it is *fully* aware and sensitive, while mankind continues to be obtuse and unkind, that could hurt nature far worse than if it remained asleep. Worse still, attempting to do such a thing outside God's will can open us to the demonic realm.

But as both Mark and I said earlier, to the extent that we are transformed into God's likeness, nature does indeed wake up to at least some of its potential. Especially vibrant with life are those trees and plants the Lord leads us to bless or touch when we go by. One can feel it powerfully in some forests and fields. A few miles southeast of Council Grove, Kansas, there is a beautiful prairie where peaceful devout Christian Kaw Indians lived for many years. Even a spiritual klutz, who normally doesn't feel anything, can walk on that land and feel goodness radiating from the fields, a presence of love and peace so encompassing that it seems like Heaven is open, and one can pray and feel his prayers being heard. Tired from stress in the ministry, I used to walk on that land and feel refreshed. Many have spoken to me of similar experiences in fields and forests. Perhaps for the same reason, Jesus went to the mountains to pray (Luke 6:12). Some places are just more alive with God's presence. But I write to say, "Won't it be wonderful when the presence of God in us sets nature free to become much more healing and refreshing for us — and a blessing to nature to be enabled and invited to minister to us as well?" Our task is to be praying that we will grow so close to Jesus that His love in us has that kind of effect on the earth around us.

In November, 1973, the Lord commanded me to write this book as the last of seven for which He gave me titles. During the intervening years I have pondered how to write it. Especially, when the sixth book, *Healing the Nations,* was completed in the year 2000, I began in earnest to plan and lay out the design and contents for *Healing the Earth*. But, each time, I got stuck. I had not yet found an answer for the skeptics whose minds were hung up on the conundrums of Isaiah 11 (of which I spoke in Chapter Seven).

And I continually asked myself, "Why did He command me to write the book, and why did He give me a burden for setting the creation free if it is all too soon, and not to be fully revealed until after Christ returns?" The answer was succinct: "In preparation." I came to understand that when a forerunner begins to receive revelations, even if he is not released to reveal what he has discovered, the way has been opened — even as no one could run a four-minute mile until Roger Bannister broke that barrier. We are corporate creatures. Haven't we all seen that many times in history when a man or woman somewhere in the world has invented something or made a discovery, almost simultaneously (or soon thereafter) others somewhere else invented or discovered something similar? Thus, though I am not permitted to know in full detail how to set the creation free, forerunning prepares the way, so that many Christians (to the extent that their character has been transformed to reflect that of Christ) will step in and quickly learn and complete what has begun.

In the meantime, what can Christians do?

First, we need to intercede for nature in prayer. Pray that destruction be stopped. Pray that people be awakened to the need to preserve what God has created. Pray that God will heal and restore what has already been damaged. One might ask, won't praying for nature take time away from praying for humans? Not at all! Historically, those who blessed nature the most through their prayers and actions have consistently been known as the most devout saints of the Church — who prayed for their fellow humans more than the rest of us do. It is true that if we make healing the earth into the latest fad, it will distract us from praying for our fellow humans. But because these saints sought after God's loving heart instead of exciting new experiences, they did not perceive prayer as a limited quantity to be parceled out. For them, drawing close to the heart of our infinite God caused the lure of time-wasting amusements to wither away. Yes, you should pray for your fellow humans first and foremost. But if you have no time left for anything else, could it be that your experience of His love has not yet surpassed the stimulation you feel watching T.V. and playing video games? Saints who learn to sit and soak in the lap of our loving Father

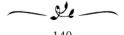

find that their own love is multiplied, until there is more than enough time to pray for all aspects of God's creation.

Second, as God prompts, we can heal specific animals, places, objects, lands and nations, even though we cannot awaken the entire creation before God's appointed time. How fervently I yearn for Christians around the world to learn how to heal nature's wounds! Not merely in compassion for all the aspects that suffer needlessly when we fail to heal, but because the way will be progressively prepared for that day when Christ returns, and God releases His own into the freedom that, in the new Earth, will set all of creation free.

As I said earlier, since nature abhors a vacuum (and Christians have failed to occupy the field) New Agers have entered and defiled so much that many Christians have become leery of entering — for fear of becoming, or being falsely labeled as, New Agers. Throughout this book, I have said that our mindsets about nature will require paradigm shifts toward a more biblical understanding, and the courage to risk. We need not fear making mistakes. Of course we will. We don't enter any field of discovery without making mistakes. But under the guidance of the Holy Spirit, accountability to the church, and a solid foundation of scriptural principles, we can learn wisdom as we go.

Though I have taught many "how-tos" in this book, my purpose is not to hand down a finished manual. It is to call us all into the enterprise of healing and discovery that will result in a maturing people being called by God as His sons to set the creation free, to whatever extent is possible in the present age. My purpose is to prepare for and hasten that day.

A **third** thing we can do is to understand that there are

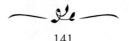

principles that are groundwork for any ministry, but especially in this particular area. One principle is humility. As I said earlier, my Osage ancestors thought of all animals as their little brothers and sisters to be cared for and loved. Behind that was a level of honor and respect far more in line with Scripture than today's mentality, which, as I said earlier, is typified by the thinking of the seventeenth century Enlightenment philosopher, Rene Descartes. L.S. Heamshaw writes, "To Descartes, man alone possessed consciousness and thought; all lower animals were merely machines. It was not that brutes have less reason than man, but that they have none at all." What this implies is that animals may be treated like machines.

That arrogant way of thinking and relating to animals (and to all of God's creation) must stop! All the ways Descartes' worldview has lodged in us must die on the cross of Christ!

We need to ask for a new heart that respects and honors God's creation.

Fourth, we must desist from callously using, manipulating, exploiting and wasting the earth's resources, excusing ourselves that "we have that right, because God has given us dominion over the creation." We were not given that right! God's declaration that we are to have dominion (Genesis 1:26), needs to be comprehended in light of the Christian sense of what "lordship" means. The Bible says:

Jesus called them to Himself and said, "You know that the

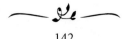

rulers of the gentiles lord it over them, and their great men exercise authority over them. It is not this way among you, but whoever wishes to become great among you shall be your servant, and whoever wishes to be first among you shall be your slave" (Matthew 20:25-27).

Look at how God expresses this attitude toward animals. When Jonah wanted God to destroy Nineveh, God replied: "Should I not have compassion on Nineveh, the great city in which there are more than 120,000 persons who do not know the difference between their right and left hand, **as well as many animals**" (Jonah 4:11, emphasis added)? Here, God expresses the same loving concern for animals as He does for small children (who do not yet know the difference between right and left) — not to mention the adults of Nineveh. When the sins of the Israelites brought war upon the land, God promised to restore to the animals the safety this had deprived them of: "In that day **I will also make a covenant for them with the beasts of the field, the birds of the sky and the creeping things of the ground.** And I will abolish the bow, the sword and war from the land, and will make them lie down in safety" (Hosea 2:18, emphasis added).

God ordered a Sabbath rest, not only for humans but also for animals, *so that your ox and your donkey may rest* (Exodus 23:12, NIV). When Israel was carried off to Babylon, God gave the land the Sabbath rests the people had deprived it of: "**The land enjoyed its Sabbath rests**; all the time of its desolation it rested, until the seventy years were completed in fulfillment of the word of the LORD spoken by Jeremiah" (2

Chronicles 36:21, NIV, emphasis added).

God commanded us to treat animals as kindly as He does. Every seventh year, during the land's Sabbath rest, the Israelites were to leave the land unplowed, and the vineyard and olive tree were not to be harvested, "…so that the needy of your people may eat; and **whatever they leave the beast of the field may eat**" (Exodus 23:11:b, emphasis added). Deuteronomy 25:4 commands farmers, "**Do not muzzle an ox while it is treading out the grain.**" In other words, do not torture it with hunger by withholding straw even as it works to separate it from the grain. So important is kindness to animals that it is even said to be one of the telling marks of a righteous man! "**A righteous man cares for the needs of his animal**, but the kindest acts of the wicked are cruel" (Proverbs 12:10, NIV, emphasis added). This adds another dimension to why Proverbs 22:2 says, "The wicked will be cut off from the land and the treacherous will be uprooted from it."

Do you see how important is the call to treat the earth with dignity and respect? Our culture's way of thinking may tempt you to regard this merely as a nice thing to do, but not at all primary to the Christian lifestyle. This could not be farther from the truth! Respect and loving care for the earth is a key part of the very mandate to walk in the nature and character of our Lord! Far from giving us the right to exploit nature, dominion calls us to serve the creation so that it may become all that God intends it to be. When we serve nature, nature responds in kind.

For instance, a fifteen year-old saint from Asia Minor named Mamas, who lived in the late third century, was so loving and gentle that wild goats and a doe allowed him to milk them,

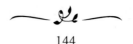

144

and many other animals gathered around him. When he was thrown into prison for refusing to worship the Roman idols, a dove brought food to his cell, which Mamas multiplied for his fellow prisoners like Christ's loaves and fishes. Later, he was sent to be torn apart by wild beasts in the Roman arena. But a bear only laid down and hugged his feet. A leopard hugged and kissed his neck and wiped off his sweaty brow. When a lion was set loose on Mamas, it turned out to be one that had he had befriended in the wilderness. Witnesses said that just like Balaam's donkey, it spoke aloud through a human voice, saying, "You are the shepherd who attended me on the mountain!" Then it leaped into the crowd and mauled many of the people who had come to cheer on Mamas' death. A week later an even more ferocious lion was let loose upon him, but it only laid at his feet. Emperor Aurelian finally gave up trying to send animals against him, and had him stoned to death instead.[73] Such was the case for many of Christian martyrs throughout the Roman Empire. The animals sensed their purity and the presence of God around them, and often refused to harm them.

In the fifth or sixth century, a Welsh saint named Tydecho had a relationship with wild animals similar to that of Mamas. A local chieftain named Maelgwyn Gwynedd wanted to cause difficulty for Tydecho, so he gave him some valuable white horses to take care of, knowing that he would allow them to frolic in the wind and rain. By the time he demanded them back, as he had expected, kind Tydecho had allowed them to roam wild and become unkempt. Maelgwyn used this as pretense

---

[73] Stefanatos, Joanne, D.V.M., *Animals and Man: a State of Blessedness* (Minneapolis, MN: Light and Life Publishing Co., 1992), 225-234.

to take vengeance by confiscating Tydecho's oxen to prevent him from plowing his land. But the wild animals remembered Tydecho's kindness, and repaid him for it. Stags let themselves be harnessed to the plow, and then a wolf came from the forest and let itself be used to draw the harrow to break up the clods they left behind.[74]

These are, of course, exceptional examples; few Christians have had this kind of redemptive effect upon nature. But that does not mean that we can never walk like Mamas and Tydecho. As Mark said in Chapter One, sainthood is not a luxury for the few. We are all called to be saints. But before we can walk like these two men walked, we must understand that mastership in God's kingdom means laying down one's life for others — our fellow human beings as well as all of God's animals, plants, objects and lands, so that the creation may become more and more glorious in the way God intends.

As I have said, we are not inveighing against any and all use of nature's resources, such as mining, logging, farming, fishing, or even hunting and killing. Our Lord was the first to kill animals when He made clothing from animal skins for Adam and Eve (Genesis 3:21). And when Noah stepped out of the ark, God told him, "Every moving thing that is alive shall be food for you" (Genesis 9:3a). The resurrected Christ ate fish (Luke 24:42-43). The Lord's temple was adorned with carvings made of cedar, logged in Lebanon (1 Kings 5:10; 6:18).

We **are** saying that stewardship must become primary as we care for the earth. As Mark said earlier, so many writers and

---

[74.] Stefanatos, Joanne, D.V.M., *Animals and Man: a State of Blessedness* (Minneapolis, MN: Light and Life Publishing Co., 1992), 225-234.

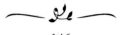

teachers have spoken of good stewardship in the husbanding of earth's resources that we don't need to repeat such teachings, or to "re-invent the wheel." What we would add is that we must learn how to involve the Holy Spirit's sensitivity in our decision-making relative to stewardship. No attitude or way of thinking (such as greed, selfish desire or ambition) can be allowed to guide us, other than the Holy Spirit. I gave an example earlier — listening to the Lord to discern strategies for harvesting lumber. But again, understand that my saying the Holy Spirit is to guide us is not to devalue scientific research; it is rather to enlist His help as He speaks to us through both research and the gifts of the Spirit.

A **fifth**, and perhaps the most important thing we can do to heal the earth, is to **love** the creation — all its animals, plants, objects and lands. Farmers have spoken to me of love for their lands. Many people have testified to Paula and me of their love for their plants, as well as their pets. They have testified of knowing how their plants become lonely if they ignore them or are away from home for a long time. Our daughter-in-law, Maureen, dearly loves plants and has a green-thumb par excellence. When she and Mark were preparing to move from Florida to Idaho, for the first time ever, her plants began to droop (although she continued her usual care) as if they somehow sensed that they would soon be left behind by the woman who had so loved and cared for them.

Are these people all fooling themselves? Are they imputing to plants what, in reality, is their own human feelings? Most to whom I have spoken have insisted that what they

Healing The Earth

sense is objective reality. They may have scriptural warrant. I have already cited many scriptures throughout the Bible which speak of nature — trees, pastures, hills, floods, etc. — reacting emotionally over the events of mankind. Here are a few more:

Shout for joy, O heavens, for the Lord has done it!
Shout joyfully, you lower parts of the earth.
Break forth into a shout of joy, you mountains,
O forest, and every tree in it;
For the Lord has redeemed Jacob,
And in Israel He shouts forth His glory.

Isaiah 44:23

Shout for joy, O heavens! And rejoice, O earth!
Break forth into joyful shouting, O mountains!
For the Lord has comforted His people
And will have compassion on His afflicted.

Isaiah 49:13

For you will go out with joy
And be led forth with peace:
The mountains and the hills will break
forth into shouts of joy before you,
And all the trees of the field will clap their hands.
Instead of the thorn bush the cypress will come up,
And it will be a memorial to the Lord
For an everlasting sign that shall not be cut off.

Isaiah 55:12-13

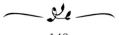

148

The Depths Of The Problem: Part Three

Of course, not every word of this is literal. Trees do not literally have "hands," and mountains do not literally "shout." But can we also say that no literal joy is being expressed? If so, there is nothing that "clapping hands" and "shouting" figuratively allude to.

The Hebrew people expected all of nature — especially trees, mountains and hills — to rejoice along with them, and they also expected that their sins would cause earth to mourn:

> *The Lord roars from Zion,*
> *And from Jerusalem He utters His voice;*
> *And the shepherds' pasture grounds mourn,*
> *And the summit of Carmel dries up.*
>
> Amos 1:2

> *How long is the land to mourn*
> *And the vegetation of the countryside to wither?*
> *For the wickedness of those who dwell in it,*
> *Animals and birds have been snatched away,*
> *Because men have said, "He will not see our latter ending."*
>
> Jeremiah 12:4

For too long we have thought non-corporately, as though what we do privately has no affect upon anyone or anything else. Scripture makes it undeniable (if we can believe His Word) that everything we do is woven into the fabric of all nature and all mankind. There is no private sin, however secret. And there is no private rejoicing, even if what we rejoice about is unknown to others. Nature rejoices with us empathetically, and it mourns with and for us when we go astray.

I say, prophetically, that when enough Christians catch this message and begin to relate to plants, objects and lands around them with the same love as for their pets, we will see nature (at least within each of our limited spheres of influence) begin to respond in kindness as never before — provided that our lives reflect the nature of Christ. Nature longs to be loved. It hurts in loneliness and grief when we are callous and uncaring.

A **sixth** discipline we can enter, with regard to ministry to the earth, is to study the Bible in relation to all it has to say about nature. If we read with expectancy, breaking free from old habits of glossing over and not seeing, we will find riches that enlarge our perspectives, mushroom our hearts' feelings about the earth, and heighten our spirits' sensitivities far beyond where we are now. Searching the Word for expressions about animals, plants, objects and lands will also prepare our hearts to act with less stumbling and error, as the Lord increasingly enables us to set nature free.

We can pray for our Lord to open our eyes when we read familiar passages like Psalm 148. Try it. Pray first for the Lord to open your heart and give you new eyes, and then read this psalm again (which I quoted in Chapter Two):

Praise the Lord!
Praise the Lord from the heavens:
Praise Him in the heights!
Praise Him, all His angels:
Praise Him, all His hosts!
Praise Him, sun and moon;

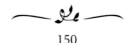

The Depths Of The Problem: Part Three

Praise Him, all stars of light!
Praise Him, highest heavens,
And the waters that are above the heavens!
Let them praise the name of the Lord,
For He commanded, and they were created.
He has also established them forever and ever;
He has made a decree which shall not pass away.

Praise the Lord from the earth,
Sea monsters and all deeps,
Fire and hail, snow and clouds,
Stormy wind fulfilling His word,
Mountains and all hills,
Fruit trees and all cedars,
Beasts and all cattle,
Creeping things and winged fowl,
Kings of the earth and all peoples,
Princes and all judges of the earth,
Both young men and virgins,
Old men and children.

Let them praise the name of the Lord,
For His wisdom is exalted;
His glory is above earth and heaven.
And He has lifted up a horn for His people.
Praise for all His godly ones;
Even for the sons of Israel, a people near to Him.
Praise the Lord!

Healing The Earth

What a marvelous psalm! But did you read it with old eyes, glossing over the psalmist's speaking directly to nearly all aspects of God's creation, expecting each to "hear" and "obey"? Did you see that he expected all aspects of the creation to be able to worship the Lord? Or were those words mere poetic language to you? Did you see that he addressed both animate and inanimate aspects with the same expectancy, calling all alike to worship and praise the Lord? In the same sentence, he spoke to humans, "sea monsters" (living animals) and "fire and hail" (inanimate objects). In the same sentence, without distinction, he spoke to the tame and the wild — "Beasts and all cattle," the cultivated and the uncultivated — "Fruit trees and all cedars."

We were trained in the world's way of thinking before we came to know Jesus, so we could have expected God to draw some careful delineations: "Okay, I know that humans and animals have spirits (Ecclesiastes 3:21) and that inanimate things like clouds don't, so I'm recognizing that and speaking differently to each of them." But the psalmist, under the Holy Spirit's anointing, makes no such distinction. Because we humans have a mind, a will and a personal spirit, and we alone are made in God's image, we are, of course, in a variety of ways more capable of worshipping God than animals and inanimate things. But the Holy Spirit still calls both into praise and worship. We must come to see that each aspect of God's creation is somehow "aware" and responsive — each in its own unexplained way and degree, and somehow capable of worshipping God — and respect that.

We are indeed the highest of all of God's earthly creations

and are of more value. The Lord Himself said so: "So do not fear, you are of more value than many sparrows" (Matthew 19:31). And in Matthew 12:12 He said, "How much more valuable then, is a man than a sheep!" But value does not justify pride or lording it over any aspect of nature. We must see that if we would relate effectively to all parts of the Lord's Kingdom, it must be through humility. Adam's being lord over Eve did not mean he had license to use her as his slave. Rather, he was to serve her and lay down his life for her.

In the same way, we must stop relating from an attitude of haughty superiority toward pets, wild animals, plants or any objects of God's creation. Our high status is not something we merit by our own efforts. I can testify from experience on our small farm and my grandfather's ranch that the creation and its animals can sense and react to those whose attitudes exalt them above others. By their actions I have seen otherwise gentle animals rebuke the prideful.

Look again at the story of Balaam's ass in Numbers 22, whose mouth was opened to speak to the erring prophet, and who could reason and present her case better than some lawyers! Ponder how seven pairs of clean creatures and two of all the unclean entered the ark. Noah could not have found and corralled such a host! The animals must have been able to hear God command them to travel long distances to Noah's location, and not to harm each other along the way, nor to attack Noah and his family upon their arrival.

A **seventh** thing we can do to heal the earth — and one of the most important — is to enter with others, as the Lord directs, into investigating the history of lands, and to follow the Holy Spirit as He reveals how to "heal" plots of ground, areas, regions and entire nations. I testified of this in several stories in previous chapters. This is major. I have not taught fully in this book about all the principles regarding the healing of lands because many Holy Spirit-filled Christians have already become adept in the transformation of small and large areas of the earth, and because I wrote more fully about this in our book, *Healing the Nations*. But let not a lack of many teachings and stories here be taken to indicate lack of importance. Lands on which wars have been fought reek with need. "Your brother's blood cries out to me from the ground" (Genesis 4:10, NIV). The healing of lands on which tragedies and violence have occurred is perhaps the most needful part of our calling to heal the earth in preparation for the Lord's return.

Finally, I have delayed finishing this book because until now it has not seemed that the Body of Christ had matured sufficiently. I began to teach about these things more than thirty years ago, and the reactions of most were either disbelief or attack. Many Christians were not at all prepared to receive testimonies and revelations so far outside their comfort zones. The Lord warned me not to cast pearls before swine (Matthew 7:6). (Not that people are swine; Jesus was using an idiom of speech common in the culture of that day. A "swine of the mind" was a rapacious and skeptical way of thinking and reacting which could cause people to turn heedlessly and rend those who spoke.) I learned the hard way that, during the early days of the charismatic movement, there were many "swines of the mind." But it has been amazing to me how the Lord has been so rapidly maturing many of His people! I have found that many are now hearing and receiving what, years before, they would have rejected and castigated mindlessly. At the same time I am trusting that they are learning to test by the standards of Scripture any idea that is new to them. In releasing this book, I am trusting not only the Lord, but the rising magnanimity of mind and maturity among many in the Body of Christ.

This gives me hope. Can the rapid maturation of some mean also that our Lord will increasingly release us to set the creation free to whatever extent is possible before Christ's return? We fervently hope so. "For we know that the whole creation groans and suffers the pains of childbirth together until now" (Romans 8:22).

But let me caution that receiving this knowledge does not, by itself, lead to the kind of maturity of which I speak. Throughout history, those who brought transformation to the earth were never the merely knowledgeable. Rather, they were always ones the church recognized as leading exemplary lives, filled with prayer, repentance, devotion to the word, and constant intimacy with our Lord Jesus Christ.

What will transform nature around us? Our own transformation!

As Paula and I have said again and again throughout the books we have written, transformation is not a one-time experience. Those who think it is, often quote Paul as saying that we are "new creatures" in Christ because God has reconciled us to Himself (2 Corinthians 5:17, 19). But that is not the end of our transformation. It is the beginning, for Paul goes on to say, "Therefore…we beg you on behalf of Christ, **be reconciled to God**" (verse 20, NAS, emphasis added). Make no mistake; unless you are living a lifelong lifestyle of repentance, you will hardly be reconciled, and will see limited transformation in this life.

Again, Mark and I challenge you to ask yourself, "Am I being transformed?" "Am I walking as Jesus walked?" "Does my life increasingly display the fruits of the Spirit?" "Do people feel closer to Jesus after being with me?" Having read this book, you might also ask, "Is my spirit able to be refreshed by God's good earth?" "Is the earth blossoming around me?" "Does it yield its produce for me?" "Are animals, both tame and wild, loving and gentle in my presence?"

2 Corinthians 3:18 says, "But we all, with unveiled face, beholding as in a mirror the glory of the Lord, are being transformed into the same image from glory to glory, just as from the Lord, the Spirit." As Mark suggested in Chapter One, the extent to which the creation is transformed by your presence may be a good measure of the extent to which you have been transformed! An episode in the life of St. Makarios the Roman,[75] who lived sometime in the first few centuries, poignantly illustrates this. Each day two lions came to his home to keep him company. But one night Makarios chose to indulge lustful thoughts (the story does not disclose exactly how). He realized how far he had fallen when he noticed that for the next ten days, the lions refused to come near him. When he repented

---

[75.] **Note:** not to be confused with Macarius the Roman of Novgorod, Russia, who lived in the 1500's.

[76.] Lysicatos, Soterios, "The Saints and the Animals," *Orthodox Theology, Saints and the Animals*, http://orthodox-world.pblogs.gr/2008/06/orthodox-theology-saints-and-the-animals-a-pre-fall-picture.html, 2011 (accessed July 15, 2012).

they returned and again became his companions.[76] This story is not as well historically attested as some. But no matter whether it is legend or fact, it reveals that those who handed it down to us understood that nature will respond to nothing less than a life given completely to Jesus.

If people use the information in this book merely as a "tool" for changing the natural world without resolving to pursue a life of holiness, this knowledge will be nothing more than the latest toy in childish hands, and will yield little fruit for the kingdom. But we have faith that there are those who are answering God's call to grow in radical commitment to our Savior, and are thus increasingly prepared to bless the earth, whose spiritual health is so readily affected by our own.

Oh, may that time come quickly! The earth, and mankind, both desperately need His healing and restoration, especially as many men's love grows ever colder, and wickedness continues to foment wars and destruction. May God quickly mature His people (at least a sufficient remnant). And may this book be at least one small drop in an ocean of preparedness which shall hasten that day when Christ will return and say, "Now! Let's reveal the sons of God and set the creation free. It's time!"

Bibliography

Albrecht, Mark C., Reincarnation: *A Christian Critique of a New Age Doctrine*, Downers Grove, IL, Intervarsity Press, 1982.

Arseniev, Nicholas, *Mysticism and the Eastern Church*, Crestwood, NY, St. Vladimir's Seminary Press, 1979.

Attenborough, David, "Wild Crows Inhabiting the City Use it to their Advantage," *BBC Wildlife*, video clip, *Youtube*, 2007, accessed June 30, 2012.

Boys, Richard C., Ralph Cohen, Vinton A. Dearing and Lawrence Clark Powell, editors, *Theologia Ruris, Sive Schola Et Scalla Naturae* (The Book of Nature), Los Angeles, CA, William Andrews Clark Memorial Library and the University of California, 1956.

Clayton, Nicola and Nathan Emory, "Corvid Cognition," *Academic.edu*, 2012, accessed July 18, 2012,   http://qmul.academia.edu/NathanEmery/Papers/226987/Corvid_Cognition.

Dao, Christine, "Man of Science, Man of God: George Washington Carver," *Institute For Creation Research*, 2008, accessed Oct. 26, 2012, www.icr.org/article/science-man-god-george-washington-carver/.

Demello, Margo, "Yips, Barks and Chirps, The Language of Prairie Dogs," *Petroglyphs*, 2007 accessed Feb. 1, 2013, http://www.petroglyphsnm.org/wildsides/pdlanguage.html.

"Dolphins Identify Themselves with Names," *Softpedia*, 2001-2013, accessed Jan. 31, 2013, http://news.softpedia.com/news/Dolphins-Identify-Themselves-with-Names-23078.shtml.

"Dolphin Sounds and Acoustics," *Dolphin Facts and Information*, 2012, accessed Jan. 31, 2013, http://www.dolphins-world.com/Dolphins_Sounds_and_Acoustics.html.

"Emanation," *New Testament Made Easy*, 2011, accessed July 6, 2012, http://www.newtestamentmadeeasy.com/emanation.html.

"Ethiopian Girl Reportedly Guarded by Lions," *Associated Press*, June 21, 2005, accessed Jan. 24, 2012, http://www.msnbe.msn.com/id/8305836/ns/world_news-africa/t/ethiopian-girl-reportedly-guardedlions/#.TyA1_aWJcmY.

Feister, John, "Stories About St. Francis and the Animals," *Seasonal Features, St. Francis of Assisi, AmericanCATHOLIC.org,* 1996-2012, accessed July 7, 2012, http://www.americancatholic.org/features/francis/stories.asp#bir.

Ghezzi, Bert, *Mystics and Miracles*, Chicago, IL, Loyola Press, 2002.

"George Washington Carver Biography," *bio.truestory*, accessed July 6, 2012, http://www.biography.com/articles/George-Washington-Carver-9240299.

"George Washington Carver Quotes," *blackmissouri*, 2008, accessed July 6, 2012, http://www. blackmissouri.com/digest/george-washington-carver-quotes.html.

"George Washington Carver," *The Great Idea Finder*, 2006, accessed July 6, 2012, http://www.ideafinder.com/history/inventors/carver.htm.

Guroian, Vigen, *Inheriting Paradise, Meditations on Gardening*, Grand Rapids MI, Wm. B. Eerdman's Publishing Co., 1999.

Hearnshaw, L.S., *Discourse on Method* New York, NY, Routledge and Kegan Paul, 1987.

"Hieromartyr Artemon the Presbyter of Laodicea in Syria," *Orthodox Church in America*, accessed July 16, 2012, http://ocafs.oca.org/FeastSaintsLife.asp?FSID=101072.

Jacobs, Bill, "My Brothers, Birds, You should Praise Your Creator," *St. Francis of Assisi, Blessed Kateri Tekakwitha Conservation Center,* 2000-2012, accessed January 2, 2012, http://www.conservation.catholic.org, /st_francis_of_assisi. htm.

"Job 31:38," *Biblios.com,* accessed July 7, 2011, http://www.scripturetext.com/job/31-38.htm.

Josephus, Flavius, *The Works of Josephus,* translated by William Whiston, Peabody, MA, Hendrickson Publishers, 1989.

Keselopoulos, Anestis G., *Man and His Environment,* Crestwood, NY, St. Vladimir's Seminary Press, 2001.

Liester, Mitchell B., M.D., "George Washington Carver, Scientist and Mystic," *customer. hbci.com,* accessed October 4, 2012, http://customers.hbci.com/~wenonah/new/g-carver.htm.

Lysicatos, Soterios, "The Saints and the Animals," *Orthodox Theology, Saints and the Animals, a Pre-fall Picture,* 2011, accessed July 15, 2012, http://orthodoxworld. pblogs.gr/2008/06/orthodox-theology-saints-and-the-animals-a-pre-fall-picture.html.

Markides, Kyriacos C., *The Mountain of Silence,* New York, NY, Random House, Inc., 2002.

Marshall, Peter and David Manuel, *The Light and the Glory,* Old Tappan, NJ, Fleming H. Revell Co., 1977.

"Martyr Zoticus of Constantinople, Feeder of Orphans, (4th c.)," *holytrinityorthodox. com,* accessed July 16, 2012, http://www.holytrinityorthodox.com/calendar/los/December/31-04.htm.

McClosky, Fr. Pat, O.F.M., "Where Did St. Francis Say That?" *St. Anthony Messenger Ask a Franciscan, AmericanCATHOLIC.org,* 1996, accessed Aug. 28, 2012, http://www.americancatholic.org/messenger/oct2001/Wiseman.asp.

McMullen, Emerson Thomas, "George Washington Carver and Other Christians Who Were Scientists," *oocities.org,* 1999, accessed October 27, 2012, http://www. oocities.org/etmcmullen/CARVER.htm.

Mileant, Bishop Alexander,"St. Seraphim of Sarov," *St. Seraphim of Sarov Life and Teachings,* translated by Nicholas and Natalia Semyanko, *OrthodoxPhotos. com,* 2003-2012, accessed July 7, 2012, http://www.orthodoxphotos.com/readings/SOS/.

Pratney, Winkie, *Healing the Land,* Grand Rapids, MI, Chosen Books, 1993.

Saia, Carol, "God Ends Idol's 700-year Reign in Almolonga, Guatemala," *GlowTorch,* 2009, accessed July 14, 2012, http://www.glowtorch.org/Home/IdolatryendsinAlmolonga/tabid/2767/Default.aspx.

Schaeffer, Francis and Udo Middelmann, *Pollution and the Death of Man,* Wheaton, Il., Tyndale Publishing, 1970.

Schlink, Mother Basilea, *A Matter of Life and Death,* Darmstadt-Everstadt, Germany, Evangelical sisterhood of Mary, 1974.

Schlink, Mother Basilea, *Repentance, the Joy Filled Life,* Minneapolis, MN, Bethany House Publishers, 1968.

Stefanatos, Joanne, D.V.M., *Animals and Man: a State of Blessedness,* Minneapolis, MN, Light and Life Publishing Co.,1992.

Stefanatos Joanne, D.V.M., *Animals Sanctified, a Spiritual Journey,* Minneapolis, MN, Light and Life Publishing Co., 2001.

St. Seraphim of Sarov, *Little Russian Philokalia,* Vol. 1, Platina, CA, St. Herman of Alaska Press, 1978.

"The Tales of the Prairie Dog," *Now I Know,* 2012 accessed Feb. 1, 2013, http://nowiknow.com/the-tales-of-the-prairie-dog/.

Velimirovic, St. Nicholai, *The Prologue of Ohrid*, Vols. 1 & 2, Alhambra, CA, Serbian Orthodox Diocese of North America, 2002.

Vine, W. E., M.A., *Vine's Expository Dictionary of New Testament Words*, Iowa Falls, IA, Riverside Book and Bible House, 1940.

Uitenbogaard, Arie, "Meaning and Etymology of the Hebrew Name, Anah," *Abarim Publications*, accessed February 17, 2012, http://www.abarimpublications. com/Meaning/Anah.html#TzlQicWJcmY

Wochoven, Natalie, "How Long Until We Learn Animal Languages?" *BETA News*, 2012, accessed Feb. 1, 2013, http://www.petroglyphsnm.org/wildsides/pdlanguage. html.

Yong, Ed, "When Meeting up at Sea, Bottlenose Dolphins Exchange Name-Like Whistles," *Discover, The Magazine of Science, Technology and the Future*, 2012, accessed Jan. 31, 2013, http://blogs.discovermagazine.com/ notrocketscience/2012/02/28/when-meeting-up-at-sea-bottlenose-dolphins- exchange-name-like-whistles/#.UQwfUx1X2pY.

About The Authors

John Sandford

John and his wife, Paula, are considered pioneers in both the prophetic and inner healing movements. Together they founded Elijah House Ministries in Coeur d' Alene, Idaho in 1974. This ministry seeks to fulfill the "Elijah Task" (as reflected, for instance, in Malachi 4:5-6: Elijah will "...turn the hearts of fathers to their children and children to their fathers" by raising up "prayer ministers"—Christian laymen and women who address others' personal and interpersonal issues through "inner healing." This Holy Spirit-led ministry features not only active listening, but, most importantly, prayers of confession, repentance, forgiveness and resurrection into new life. Elijah House has also done extensive work reconciling people groups. In fulfillment of Matthew 17:11, Elijah House also seeks to help fulfill the Elijah task of "restoring all things," including the proper use of the prophetic gift, and—as regards this book—healing the earth, among other subjects. What started as two people working out of their house has mushroomed to include hundreds of lay workers around the world, and ministry centers in many nations.

Other titles John has authored include *Elijah Among Us, Healing the Nations* and *Why Good People Mess Up.* He and Paula have co-authored *Restoring the Christian Family, Transforming the Inner man, God's Power to Change, Letting Go of Your Past, Growing pains, The Elijah Task* and *Prophets, Healers and the Emerging Church.* With Lee Bowman they have also co-authored *Choosing Forgiveness* and *Waking the*

Slumbering Spirit. With his son, Loren, John has co-authored *Renewal of the Mind.* Paula has authored *Healing Victims of Sexual Abuse* and *Healing for a Woman's Emotions.*

After earning a master of divinity in religion and personality, John pastored churches in Illinois, Kansas and Idaho for twenty one years before founding Elijah House. He and Paula married in 1951. They have six children and many grandchildren and great-grandchildren.

Mark Sandford

Mark received his bachelor's degree from Boise State University in 1978 and his Master of Divinity in counseling from Denver Theological Seminary in 1985. After graduation, he served briefly as an intern prayer minister with Elijah House, then did prayer ministry in Leesburg, Florida, for three and a half years. Mark returned to Idaho and joined the Elijah House staff in 1989. In 2005, John passed the baton to Mark as Elijah House' Spiritual Director. In 2007, Paula passed her mantle to Mark's wife, Maureen.

Mark's insightful understanding of Scripture, combined with childlike faith, humility and inherent sensitivity, make him an outstanding prayer minister, teacher and international conference speaker. These same traits shine through most brilliantly in his gift of writing. With John, he co-authored *A Comprehensive Guide to Deliverance and Inner Healing.* Now, once again, he collaborates with John on *Healing the earth.*

Mark and Maureen were married in 1984 and have three children.

Elijah House

Founded by John and Paula Sandford in 1975, Elijah House consists of people from various denominations. Their common goal is restore broken relationships and to bring healing and restoration to God's broken people and to train pastors, leaders, counselors and laypersons to do the same. Elijah House also seeks to restore and refine the use of the prophetic gift, as well as other areas of life among believers. The need for these tasks is universal and without denominational boundaries, so Elijah House works to accomplish its mission through the Body of Christ, by:

Declaring principles of restoration and transformation through writing and publishing books, pamphlets, workbooks, artwork, CDs, DVDs and other materials.

Imparting principles of restoration and transformation through training pastors, leaders, counselors, lay people and concerned Christians at conferences, seminars and training events and schools, locally and around the world, and through Elijah House materials.

Applying principles of restoration and transformation through personal ministry to hundreds of individuals and families each year at Elijah House and through an international network of Elijah House-trained prayer ministers.

All that Elijah House does has one goal: to unite people with Jesus, so that all may experience the transforming power of His death and resurrection.

To contact Elijah House or to receive more information about Elijah House USA or Elijah Houses in other nations, or to receive the newsflashes and the ministry resource catalog, consult Elijah House USA's website, *www.elijahhouse.org.*

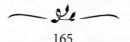

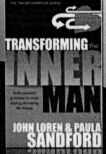

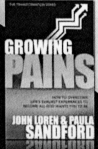

Other books by John, Paula, Mark & Loren Sandford

Transforming the Inner Man

God's Power to Change

Letting Go of Your Past

Growing Pains

The Elijah Task

Elijah Among Us

Healing the Nations

Restoring the Christian Family

Deliverance and Inner Healing

Choosing Forgiveness

Awakening the Slumbering Spirit

Healing for a Woman's Emotions

Healing Victims of Sexual Abuse

Why Good People Mess Up

Life Transformed

Understanding Prophetic Poeple

The Prophetic Church

Purifying the Prophetic

Renewal for the Wounded Warrior

Visions of the Coming Days